The Kennedys

Other Books in the History Makers Series:

The Kennedys

By Michael V. Uschan

Lucent Books
P.O. Box 289011, San Diego, CA 92198-9011

To the Marottas—Marc, Kim, Karley, Cameron, and Chloe—with all my love

Library of Congress Cataloging-in-Publication Data

Uschan, Michael V., 1948-
  The Kennedys / by Michael V. Uschan.
    p.   cm. — (History makers)
  Includes bibliographical references and index.
  ISBN 1-56006-875-2 (lib. bdg. : alk. paper)
  1. Kennedy family—Juvenile literature. 2. Presidents—United States—
Biography—Juvenile literature. 3. Statesmen—United States—Biography—
Juvenile literature. 4. Legislators—United States—Biography—Juvenile
literature. 5. Presidents' spouses—United States—Biography—Juvenile
literature. 6. Children of presidents—United States—Biography—Juvenile
literature. 7. Politicians—United States—Family relationships—Juvenile
literature. [1. Kennedy family. 2. Statesmen.]   I. Title.   II. Series.
  E176 U83   2002
  973.922'092'2—dc21   2001001159

Copyright 2002 by Lucent Books, Inc.
P.O. Box 289011, San Diego, California 92198-9011

Printed in the U.S.A.

CONTENTS

FOREWORD

The literary form most often referred to as "multiple biography" was perfected in the first century A.D. by Plutarch, a perceptive and talented moralist and historian who hailed from the small town of Chaeronea in central Greece. His most famous work, *Parallel Lives*, consists of a long series of biographies of noteworthy ancient Greek and Roman statesmen and military leaders. Frequently, Plutarch compares a famous Greek to a famous Roman, pointing out similarities in personality and achievements. These expertly constructed and very readable tracts provided later historians and others, including playwrights like Shakespeare, with priceless information about prominent ancient personages and also inspired new generations of writers to tackle the multiple biography genre.

The Lucent History Makers series proudly carries on the venerable tradition handed down from Plutarch. Each volume in the series consists of a set of six to eight biographies of important and influential historical figures who were linked together by a common factor. In *Rulers of Ancient Rome*, for example, all the figures were generals, consuls, or emperors of either the Roman Republic or Empire; while the subjects of *Fighters Against American Slavery*, though they lived in different places and times, all shared the same goal, namely the eradication of human servitude. Mindful that politicians and military leaders are not (and never have been) the only people who shape the course of history, the editors of the series have also included representatives from a wide range of endeavors, including scientists, artists, writers, philosophers, religious leaders, and sports figures.

Each book is intended to give a range of figures—some well known, others less known; some who made a great impact on history, others who made only a small impact. For instance, by making Columbus's initial voyage possible, Spain's Queen Isabella I, featured in *Women Leaders of Nations*, helped to open up the New World to exploration and exploitation by the European powers. Unarguably, therefore, she made a major contribution to a series of events that had momentous consequences for the entire world. By contrast, Catherine II, the eighteenth-century Russian queen, and Golda Meir, the modern Israeli prime minister, did not play roles of global impact; however, their policies and actions significantly influenced the historical development of both their own countries and their regional neighbors. Regardless of their relative importance in the greater historical scheme, all of the figures chronicled in the History Makers series made contributions to posterity; and their public achievements, as well as what is known about their private lives, are presented and evaluated in light of the most recent scholarship.

In addition, each volume in the series is documented and substantiated by a wide array of primary and secondary source quotations. The primary source quotes enliven the text by presenting eyewitness views of the times and culture in which each history maker lived; while the secondary source quotes, taken from the works of respected modern scholars, offer expert elaboration and/or critical commentary. Each quote is footnoted, demonstrating to the reader exactly where biographers find their information. The footnotes also provide the reader with the means of conducting additional research. Finally, to further guide and illuminate readers, each volume in the series features photographs, two bibliographies, and a comprehensive index.

The History Makers series provides both students engaged in research and more casual readers with informative, enlightening, and entertaining overviews of individuals from a variety of circumstances, professions, and backgrounds. No doubt all of them, whether loved or hated, benevolent or cruel, constructive or destructive, will remain endlessly fascinating to each new generation seeking to identify the forces that shaped their world.

The Kennedys: America's Political Royalty

A democracy since winning its freedom from England in the Revolutionary War, the United States of America has never had an official royal family. Yet when John F. Kennedy Jr. died in an airplane crash July 16, 1999, some news reports referred to this son of the nation's thirty-fifth president as "our unofficial crown prince." In *The Sins of the Father*, biographer Ronald Kessler claims Joseph Patrick Kennedy, John's grandfather, is the reason millions of Americans came to revere members of his family the way people in other countries do their kings and queens:

> By spawning America's own version of the British royal family, Kennedy founded a dynasty that produced the first Catholic president, three senators, an attorney general, three congressmen, and future presidential contenders [his grandchildren and great-grandchildren] who are likely to continue to shape American history. It was his edict that they rise, like salmon swimming upstream, to the top of American government.[1]

There have been other American political dynasties—John Adams and his son, John Quincy Adams, were both elected president, and George Bush, father and son, also captured the nation's highest office—but none as successful or powerful. In 1960, when Americans elected John Fitzgerald Kennedy president, it seemed they had voted an entire family into office when John named one brother, Robert Francis Kennedy, his attorney general, and a year later helped elect a second, Edward "Ted" Moore Kennedy, to the Senate seat he vacated to become president. Jacqueline Bouvier Kennedy brought a new sense of grace and activism to the job of First Lady, transforming the ceremonial position into one in which she took on important tasks, such as supervising a much-needed White House restoration. And the Kennedy children, John and Caroline, became symbols of the hopes and dreams all Americans had for their own sons and daughters.

Family members surround John F. Kennedy (center) in November 1960 after learning that he had been elected president.

It was their many triumphs that first brought the Kennedys to the attention of the nation and the world. But in the following decades it was a flow of much-publicized tragedies that struck members of this powerful family, as well as their own human flaws, from sexual misconduct to alcohol and drug abuse, that would heighten global fascination with anyone named Kennedy. Clare Boothe Luce, an influential political and media figure for several decades who knew the family well, once tried to explain why the Kennedys fascinated so many people:

> Where else but in gothic fiction, where else among real people, could one encounter such triumphs and tragedies, such beauty and charm and ambition and pride and human wreckage, such dedication to the best and lapses into the mire of life; such vulgar, noble, driven, generous, self-centered, loving, suspicious, devious, honorable, vulnerable, indomitable people. . . . No wonder the American public, their audience—for that matter much of the world—has been fascinated by them.[2]

The Kennedy Line

The family saga began in 1849 when Patrick Kennedy left County Wexford, Ireland for Boston, Massachusetts. Kennedy came to

America for the same reason millions of other immigrants came—the opportunity to create a better life for himself and his children. But even in his wildest dreams, this poor Irish farmer could never have imagined that his descendants would one day lead his adopted nation and make his humble family name world famous.

After graduating from Harvard University in 1912, Joseph Patrick Kennedy, Patrick's grandson, wed Rose Elizabeth Fitzgerald, another descendant of Irish immigrants, and they had nine children. A savvy and unscrupulous businessman who built a family fortune worth several hundred million dollars, Joe became a powerful figure in the Democratic Party and helped his son John become president by craftily guiding the younger Kennedy's political career starting with his first campaign for Congress in 1946.

John began his presidency by giving Americans a new sense of pride and purpose when he challenged them, in perhaps the finest inaugural speech ever given, to "ask not what your country can do for you; ask what you can do for your country."[3] Kennedy also gave his nation a new sense of hope for the future with his dramatic vow to land a man on the moon, a promise fulfilled in 1969, and his efforts to secure federal protection for African American civil rights. And he led the nation through one of its most perilous moments, the Cuban Missile Crisis in 1962, when America came closer to nuclear war with the former Soviet Union than at any other time during the long, bitter Cold War.

The Kennedy Myth

John F. Kennedy had already made a place for himself in history before his tragic death. But biographer William Manchester believes the assassin's bullet that struck him down transformed him into a mythic figure:

> Once a leader becomes a martyr, myth naturally follows. The Kennedy we knew in life vanished forever on November 22 [1963]. . . . Legends, because they are essentially tribal, override details. What the folk hero was and what he believed are submerged by the demands of those who follow him. In myth, he becomes what they want him to have been, and anyone who belittles this transformation has an imperfect understanding of truth.[4]

The myth building began after his widow compared her husband's life and death to the legendary, romantic story of King Arthur. After explaining how much the president had enjoyed lis-

John F. Kennedy is sworn in as the nation's thirty-fifth president.

tening to records of *Camelot*, a Broadway musical based on the King Arthur saga, she said:

> I realized history made Jack what he was. . . . For Jack, history was full of heroes. And if it made him this way—if it made him see the heroes—maybe other little boys will see. Men are such a combination of good and bad. Jack had this hero idea of history, the idealistic view . . . there'll never be another Camelot again.[5]

A world still mourning his death eagerly accepted the Camelot metaphor. And if John Kennedy was a king, then his entire family was royalty, which is the way the Kennedys have been perceived ever since.

CHAPTER 1

Joseph Patrick Kennedy: Founder of a Political Dynasty

When Patrick Kennedy began looking for a job after arriving in Boston, Massachusetts, on April 21, 1849, he saw signs that read: "Irish Need Not Apply." Historian James MacGregor Burns explains that in this era, Irish immigrants were discriminated against in America by Protestant businessmen and political leaders who viewed their Roman Catholic religion with suspicion:

The Irish were the lowest of the low, lower than the Germans or Scandinavians or Jews, or even the Negroes, who had come earlier and edged a bit up the economic ladder. Irishmen were lucky if they could find part-time work on the dock or in the ditch; Irish girls hoped at best to get work as maids in hotels or in the big houses on Beacon Hill. Irish transient paupers outnumbered the sum of all other nationalities. The people from Ireland were [common laborers] without machine skills or capital. Their sections of Boston were the land of the shanty Irish.[6]

Patrick Kennedy eventually found work as a cooper, mak-

Patrick J. Kennedy, the son of an Irish immigrant, started building the Kennedy fortune. His grandson would become president in 1960.

ing barrels. In 1849 he married Bridget Murphy, another Irish immigrant, and they had two daughters, Mary and Margaret, and one son, Patrick Joseph, born January 14, 1858. In November of that same year, Kennedy died of cholera in one of the epidemics that periodically swept poorer areas in big cities. Kennedy's widow took a variety of jobs to support her children and Patrick, nicknamed P. J., dropped out of school to work loading and unloading ships. He worked hard and saved his money, eventually buying several saloons and helping found a bank, the Columbia Trust Company. He also became a leader in local politics.

Kennedy wed Mary Augusta Hickey in 1887 and they had two daughters, Loretta and Mary Margaret, and a son, Joseph Patrick Kennedy, born September 6, 1888. His mother named him Joseph Patrick instead of Patrick Joseph because she believed it sounded "less Irish," which she hoped would help win her son acceptance in Boston society.

Although Joe would graduate in 1912 from prestigious Harvard University, make hundreds of millions of dollars, and become a powerful national figure in the Democratic Party, Boston's upper class continued to consider him an upstart Irishman, inferior despite his accomplishments. In 1922, for example, he was refused admission to the Cohasset (Massachusetts) Country Club. In the 1930s, when a Boston newspaper referred to him as "an Irishman," Kennedy exploded in anger: "I was born in this country. My children were born in this country. What the hell does someone have to do to become an American?"[7] His burning desire for acceptance and bitter resentment over discrimination due to his Irish heritage became twin goads that prodded him to excel in business and to push his sons to achieve even more.

A Young Entrepreneur

Though Joe grew up in luxury—the Kennedys had maids and cooks and owned a thirty-five-foot yacht—he had a ruthless ambition to make money even as a youngster. His many jobs included selling candy on a tourist boat, delivering hats for a milliner, and hawking newspapers on city streets. Joe did not need the extra cash. He simply enjoyed competing, whether in business or athletics, and he always needed to finish first; the dollars he made were like runs in baseball, a way to keep track of who was winning. In addition to his money-making ventures, Joe accompanied his father to political events, learning the practical aspects of electing candidates and dealing with government officials. His father taught him that in politics, as well as business, winning was the most important thing.

Joseph P. Kennedy in 1915, the year he was named president of Columbia Trust. His father started the bank.

Although most Irish youths attended Catholic schools, Joe's parents in 1901 sent him to Boston Latin, an elite Protestant school attended by children of Boston's leading citizens. He did well academically and starred in baseball, winning the Mayor's Cup in 1907 for his .580 batting average, the highest of any student in the city. The mayor who presented him the award was John Francis Fitzgerald, his future father-in-law.

Success—Financial and Romantic

The mayor's daughter, Rose Elizabeth Fitzgerald, was born on July 22, 1890, to a family even more prominent and politically powerful than the Kennedys. Two years later her father, who was nicknamed "Honey Fitz" for his sweet-talking manner, was elected to the Boston city council and then the state senate, where he served with Patrick Joseph Kennedy. In 1894, Fitzgerald won the first of three terms as a congressman and in 1905 was elected mayor of Boston, an office he would secure again in 1910. His victory was a major triumph for Irish-Americans in a city that had been dominated since its founding by citizens of English ancestry.

Kennedy and Fitzgerald sometimes opposed each other politically, but their families were friendly. Joe and Rose first met in 1895 during a picnic at Old Orchard Beach when he was seven and she was five. Joe began courting Rose when he entered Harvard, but the relationship progressed slowly because "Honey Fitz" opposed it. Rose was attending Manhattanville College of the Sacred Heart in Purchase, New York, from which she graduated in 1910.

Joe was also running into rejection by some Harvard classmates, who refused to let him join the most elite student groups because he was Irish. In *The Kennedys: Dynasty and Disaster*, John H. Davis explains that college scarred Joe for life:

> The result was a series of snubs from which he never fully recovered, and which gave him a complex he never lost. So painful were they, that for the rest of his life . . . he was never comfortable in the company of people not of his own [kind]. He would be wary of them, and, if he got a chance, he would get the best of them.[8]

When Kennedy graduated in 1912, his father got him a job as a state bank examiner so Joe could learn the banking business. It was knowledge Kennedy would soon put to good use. In the fall of 1913, when First Ward National, a larger Boston financial institution, began buying stock in Columbia Trust in an attempt to gain control of it, Kennedy put his son in charge of saving the family-owned bank. When the younger Kennedy raised money to buy back enough shares in Columbia to stop the takeover, his father made him its top executive at age twenty-five.

Rose Fitzgerald in 1911. Three years later she would wed Joseph P. Kennedy.

Kennedy soon began claiming he was the nation's youngest bank president, a dubious boast but one he would make for the rest of his life. Impressed by Kennedy's business success, "Honey Fitz" gave Rose permission to marry him. They were wed on October 7, 1914, by William Cardinal O'Connell.

Winning at Business

When World War I began, Kennedy left banking to manage Bethlehem Steel's shipyard in Quincy, Massachusetts. But his lust for money did not ease even then; he opened a lunchroom and sold meals to the shipyard's twenty-two thousand workers. Those profits were added to his annual salary of $20,000, a fantastic sum for that era.

After the war, Kennedy became an independent investor, speculating in stocks and business deals and making huge profits, sometimes through obtaining valuable inside information. For example, after learning that automaker Henry Ford would buy the Pond Creek Coal Company, Kennedy bought 15,000 shares of Pond stock for $16 each. When Ford purchased Pond, Kennedy sold the shares for $45 each for a profit of $675,000. (Although insider trading was a common practice in Kennedy's era, it is no longer legal to use inside information to reap huge profits.)

In college Kennedy had vowed to become a millionaire by age thirty-five, and by 1930 he was worth tens of millions of dollars. Kennedy accumulated his fortune from a variety of sources, including his purchase in 1926 of the Film Booking Office of America, an English firm that produced movies. "There are only two pursuits that get in your blood—politics and the motion picture business,"[9] said Kennedy, who in less than three years made $5 million in motion pictures. Although he made a lot of money in the stock market, he eventually doubted the stability of the nation's economy. Kennedy began selling shares in various companies before the stock market crash of October 29, 1929, which led to the Great Depression, and it is believed he made $15 million by shrewd buying and selling of stock during the market's collapse.

Allegations have also been made that in the 1920s, during Prohibition, when the manufacture and sale of alcohol was illegal, he imported liquor from overseas and sold it to organized crime figures. Frank Costello, a leader in the Mafia for decades, once claimed, "I helped Joe Kennedy get rich."[10] When Prohibition ended, Kennedy profited legally by importing liquor.

One of his biggest triumphs came in 1924 when a part owner of New York's Yellow Cab Company asked him to stop a takeover bid. Kennedy cloistered himself for weeks in hotel rooms, wheeling and dealing to stop the takeover, and when he succeeded received a huge cash payment. When he returned home after nearly a month away, Kennedy was greeted by his three-year-old daughter Eunice, who excitedly exclaimed, "Daddy, Daddy, we've got another baby."[11] He had missed the birth of Patricia, the sixth of his nine children.

A Big Family

The Kennedy clan had grown quickly after Joe and Rose were married. Joseph Patrick Jr. was born in 1915, followed by John (1917), Rosemary (1918), Kathleen (1920), Eunice (1921), Patricia (1924), Robert (1925), Jean (1928), and Edward (1932), and Kennedy was rich enough to buy several homes to house his growing brood. In 1927 he moved the family from Boston to Bronxville, a suburb of New York City, and later bought estates in Palm Beach, Florida, and Hyannis Port, Massachusetts, which became the family's favorite. It was here in the fall of 1940 that family friend Leo Damore recorded the following scenario:

Eight of the nine Kennedy children line up by age in this 1928 picture. Joe Jr. is on the far right, and John is next to him. Edward was not born until 1932.

Jack was autographing copies of *Why England Slept* while grandfather Fitzgerald was reading to him a political story from a newspaper. Young Joe was telling them something that had happened to him in Russia. Mrs. Kennedy was talking on the phone with [Francis] Cardinal Spellman. A tall and very attractive girl in a sweatshirt and dungarees turned out to be Pat, who was describing how a German Messerschmitt plane had crashed near her father's house outside [London, England]. Bobby was trying to get everybody to play charades. The next thing I knew all of us were choosing up sides for touch football and Kathleen was calling the plays in the huddle for the team I was on. There was something doing every minute.[12]

The varied activities they are engaged in paint a picture of striking accomplishment for a single family. John, known as Jack, was signing a best-selling book he had written on England's lack of preparation for World War II, a work that grew out of his senior thesis at Harvard. Joe, also a Harvard graduate and soon to become a navy pilot, had toured Europe in 1939 to assess the political situation for his father before the war began. The fact that Rose was talking to a cardinal, a very powerful figure in the Catholic Church, showed how important the Kennedys were. Pat's story was about her father, who was at the time U.S. ambassador to Great Britain.

One of the Kennedys not mentioned was Rosemary, who was born mildly retarded. A year after this gathering she would be placed in St. Coletta's, a Catholic nursing home in Jefferson, Wisconsin, where she still resided in 2001. Rosemary's condition was manageable while she was growing up, but when she became more uncontrollable as an adult, Joe allowed doctors to perform a prefrontal lobotomy, experimental brain surgery used to quiet violent individuals. The operation was a failure, greatly reducing Rosemary's mental capacity, and she had to be institutionalized. In later years the Kennedys would lie about Rosemary, claiming she entered St. Coletta's to teach retarded children.

The football game mentioned in this happy, energetic family scene highlights another key Kennedy characteristic—competitiveness. Eunice explains how her father instilled this trait in his children:

Even when we were six and seven years old, Daddy always entered us in public swimming races, in the different age categories so we didn't have to swim against each other. ... Daddy was always very competitive. The thing he always kept telling us was that coming in second was just no good. The important thing was to win—don't come in second or third—that doesn't count—but win, win, win.[13]

A Disjointed Family Life

Joe strived for business success with that same ferocity. And although Kennedy's money-making pursuits often kept him away from home, John always thought he was a good dad:

> My father wasn't around as much as some fathers when I was young. But whether he was there or not, he made his children feel that they were the most important things in the world to him. He held up standards for us, and he was very tough when we failed to meet those standards.[14]

When Kennedy was home, he would grill his children during dinner about their daily activities and debate news events, especially politics; while away on business Kennedy would telephone often or write letters. And his involvement with the movie industry had fringe benefits for his children, like the time cowboy hero Tom Mix sent the two oldest Kennedy boys pairs of chaps, the protective leggings cowboys wear. "Joe and Jack," said Rose, "ran around with those chaps on and all the neighborhood boys were very envious of them."[15]

Joe, however, was not the only parent gone a lot. His wife was nicknamed "Rambling Rose" for her many trips to Europe to buy clothes—starting in 1929, she traveled there seventeen times in seven years. A devout Catholic, Rose was also away often while participating in church-related activities. John, who was twelve when her travels commenced, once bitterly criticized her: "My mother was either at some Paris fashion house or else on her knees in some church. She was never there when we really needed her. My mother never really held me and hugged me. Never. Never!"[16]

The prolonged absences meant the children were usually cared for by servants, and they were also dispatched to boarding schools as soon as they were old enough. Thus the Kennedys experienced a disjointed home life, one that was not always happy or full of much love.

Tension also existed between Joe and Rose because he pursued other women, and shortly before Patricia's birth in 1924 Rose became so angry that she left him. After three weeks, her father convinced her to go home: "You've made your commitment, Rosie, and you must honor it now."[17] Rose returned to a humiliating home life, but she would make her husband pay for his infidelities. Rose once commented to a friend that she was able to get anything

Joseph P. Kennedy and his wife, Rose. Their marriage suffered because of Kennedy's infidelity.

she wanted from Joe by being "icy": "Clothes, jewels, everything. You have to know how to use that iciness."[18]

Kennedy generally kept his relationships with other women private, but his affair with Gloria Swanson, the most glamorous movie star of the 1920s, became public knowledge. He met her in 1927 and their romance became so well known that a Boston newspaper reported that Kennedy had the nation's highest private telephone bill in 1929 because he called Swanson so often. Cardinal O'Connell even arranged to meet with Swanson about the affair, reportedly telling her, "I am here to ask you to stop seeing Joseph P. Kennedy. Each time you see him it is an occasion of sin."[19] Swanson told the cardinal he should talk to Joe about the matter, not to her. They eventually split up, but Kennedy's infidelity was a glaring character defect he would pass on to his sons.

A Political Power

By 1936, Kennedy was so rich he was able to set up $10 million trust funds for each of his children. Although he would continue to increase his fortune for the rest of his life (by 1950 he was worth an estimated $400 million), Kennedy began to pursue the goal of making his family influential enough to be the equal of anyone socially. Thus he turned his attention to national politics, and in 1932 helped Franklin Delano Roosevelt win his first presidential election.

After making a $50,000 contribution and using his financial and political connections to help the New York governor defeat Republican president Herbert Hoover, Kennedy expected to be rewarded with a cabinet post. But although Roosevelt had needed his help, he did not like Kennedy, believing he was immoral and power hungry. Roosevelt made Kennedy wait more than two years, but finally on July 2, 1934, he named him the first chairman of the new Securities and Exchange Commission (SEC).

Claiming sarcastically that he wanted "to set a thief to catch a thief,"[20] Roosevelt believed Kennedy, one of the stock market's most devious manipulators, was the perfect person to put into effect the Securities Exchange Act, which empowered the government to regulate stock trading. To everyone's surprise, Kennedy did a good job. Although he held the post for only a year, Kennedy helped reform unethical stock market practices that had contributed to the nation's economic plunge. Francis P. Brassor, the first SEC secretary, praised Kennedy:

> Wall Street was scared of [the SEC]. He had the tenacity to stick with it, to talk with them, to get them to agree to regulations which, when they were first written, were highly opposed. Many of the regulations [Kennedy] fostered and promoted were self-policing. He convinced them that it was to their interest to [accept the rules]. It took a man with his courage, guts and ability.[21]

By the time Kennedy stepped down, Roosevelt was running for reelection. Kennedy hired *New York Times* reporter Arthur Krock to ghostwrite *I'm for Roosevelt*, a book in which Kennedy praised Roosevelt for saving the nation's economy. Kennedy's influence helped Roosevelt win a second term.

An Irish Ambassador

To reward Kennedy for his help, Roosevelt in January 1937 named him to head the newly created Maritime Commission, which was reforming the nation's declining commercial shipping system. It was a lesser job in the Roosevelt administration, but less than a year later the president named Kennedy to the type of position he had always desired—ambassador to Great Britain. Kennedy family biographer John H. Davis writes that the appointment gave Kennedy the social standing he so desperately wanted: "From now on, and for the rest of his life, he would be called Ambassador. The social stigma under which he had lived all his life would lift and the high status of his children and grandchildren he so ardently longed for would be virtually assured."[22]

Kennedy arrived in London in March 1938, joyous at being the first Irish-American ambassador to the country that for centuries had brutally ruled his ancestral homeland. His elation quickly vanished, however, because of a succession of diplomatic problems German dictator Adolf Hitler created in Europe. A little more than a year later on September 1, 1939, Hitler would begin World War II by invading Poland.

Like many Americans, Kennedy opposed U.S. intervention in the war. In June 1940 when he returned home for his oldest son's graduation from Harvard, he commented several times, "This is not our fight."[23] His statements infuriated the British as well as Roo-

President Franklin D. Roosevelt (seated) shakes hands with Joseph P. Kennedy after swearing him in as U.S. ambassador to England.

sevelt, who wanted to help England survive. In the summer of 1940 when German planes began bombing London nightly, Kennedy told his aide, "I'll bet you five to one—any sum—that Hitler will be at Buckingham Palace in two weeks."[24] This and other negative comments by Kennedy angered British officials, many of whom considered him a coward for spending nights in his country estate outside London to escape the air raids of the Blitz.

On October 16, 1940, Kennedy asked to be recalled from England because he was upset that Roosevelt and other State Department officials were bypassing him and corresponding directly with English prime minister Winston Churchill, who did not like or trust Kennedy. When Roosevelt did not respond, Kennedy came home anyway.

Roosevelt, however, became eager to pacify Kennedy because he needed his help to win a third campaign. Kennedy relented after they met at the White House and on October 29 gave a nationwide radio speech—he bought the air time himself for $20,000—in which he supported Roosevelt even though he disagreed with some of his policies, including Roosevelt's desire to help Great Britain. Kennedy concluded the broadcast by mentioning his family:

> My wife and I have given nine hostages to fortune. Our children and your children are more important than anything else in the world. The kind of America that they and their children will inherit is of grave concern to us all. In light of these considerations, I believe that Franklin D. Roosevelt should be reelected President of the United States.[25]

His speech helped Roosevelt win, but Kennedy resigned as ambassador December 2, 1940, and would never again hold a government post. His opposition to U.S. intervention in World War II, which continued until Japan bombed Pearl Harbor on December 7, 1941, destroyed his reputation with many Americans.

Kennedy Realizes His Dream

In his 1936 campaign book *I'm for Roosevelt*, Joseph P. Kennedy had written, "I have no political ambitions for myself or my children."[26] The statement was a blatant lie. He had long harbored a desire to become president and several times had been considered a possible candidate, but Roosevelt, who was elected four times, had always stood in his way. When Kennedy's popularity faded during World War II, he decided that he would do everything he could to elect one of his sons to the nation's highest office.

Joseph P. Kennedy with sons John (left) and Joe Jr.

His first choice was Joe Jr., but when his oldest son died while fighting in the war, he switched his focus to John. In a 1957 magazine interview, Joe candidly admitted: "I got Jack into politics. I was the one. I told him Joe Jr. was dead and that it was his responsibility to run for Congress. He didn't want to. He felt he didn't have the ability. But I told him he had to."[27]

Kennedy's financial and political backing helped John win a series of elections for the U.S. House of Representatives and Senate and he worked furiously behind the scenes in his son's 1960 presidential election. When Jack was inaugurated January 20, 1961, Joe said proudly, "This is what I've been looking forward to for a long time."[28] Kennedy family biographer Doris Kearns Goodwin writes that the founding father of this fledgling political dynasty was deeply moved that day:

> Several people reported that they saw tears glistening in his eyes [during the inaugural]. In so many ways, it was the father's triumph as well as the son's. He had not planned it this way, the second son having replaced the first, but it was surely an extraordinary end to a journey

that had begun one hundred and eleven years before when his grandfather [left Ireland].[29]

A Bitter Ending

But this proud father's moment of triumph and joy was short-lived. On December 19 of the same year his son became president, he suffered a stroke while playing golf in Palm Beach. His right side paralyzed, unable to walk, Kennedy would spend the rest of his life in a wheelchair; because his facial muscles had been damaged he also had trouble talking, with "no" the only word he could clearly enunciate.

The patriarch of the Kennedys, reduced in his final years to a powerless invalid, died November 17, 1969, two days after the last of a series of heart attacks that further weakened him. His last years were bitter ones, as he suffered not only his own devastating medical problems but the assassinations of his sons John and Robert.

Kennedy's life, however, encompassed great achievements, both his own and those of his sons. He once said, "The measure of a man's success in life is not the money he's made, it's the kind of family he raised."[30] By either measure, Kennedy had been a stunning success.

CHAPTER 2

John Fitzgerald Kennedy: The Son Who Became President

Sibling rivalries are common in large families, and the Kennedys were no exception. The fiercest battle was between the oldest sons, Joe and John. Born July 28, 1915, Joseph Patrick Kennedy Jr. built on his position of primacy by becoming a surrogate father, the big brother who even taught his siblings to swim. But Joe, who coined the nickname the "Kennedy clan," dominated his siblings physically and emotionally. An early photo shows Jack grimacing because Joe is squeezing his hand so hard, and Robert Kennedy once said, "I used to lie in my bed at night sometimes and hear the sound of Joe banging Jack's head against the wall."[31]

John Fitzgerald Kennedy was born May 29, 1917. Although Jack admired his older brother, they were intense rivals. An incident from *Triumph and Tragedy*, edited by Sidney C. Moody Jr., shows how fiercely they vied with each other as youngsters:

> The Kennedys were furious competitors and put a high premium on winning. Once young Joe and Jack decided to have a bicycle race around the block. Just a common, ordinary race? Certainly not: the two pedaled furiously in opposite directions and collided head-on at the finish line. It required twenty-eight stitches to repair Jack.[32]

Joe overshadowed Jack for many years both academically and athletically, but Jack finally topped him by writing a best-selling book and in World War II surpassed him again by becoming a hero. When Joe died on a dangerous mission while trying to match his younger brother's valor, their father ordered Jack to replace Joe in his plan to make the Kennedys so powerful, no one would ever snub them again. Jack once admitted there was nothing he could do about his father's command: "It was like being drafted. My father wanted his eldest son in politics. 'Wanted' isn't the right word. He *demanded* it."[33]

A Youth Filled with Illness

The stitches Jack received after his disastrous bicycle race with Joe were just one of many medical emergencies he endured while growing up, including bouts with whooping cough, measles, and chicken pox. In 1920 at the age of three, Jack was hospitalized for scarlet fever and given the last rites, the Roman Catholic sacrament for those near death. Robert once said:

> At least one half of the days that he spent on earth were days of intense physical pain. He had almost every conceivable ailment. When we were growing up together, we used to laugh about the great risk a mosquito took in biting Jack Kennedy—with some of his blood the mosquito was almost sure to die.[34]

Jack's illnesses led him to love reading, a trait he shared with another president who was sickly as a child, Theodore Roosevelt. He enjoyed history books and adventure tales like *The Arabian Nights*, and his wife, Jacqueline, once said that to understand her husband, "You must think of him as this little boy, sick so much of the time, reading in bed, reading history, reading the *Knights of the Round Table*."[35]

In 1930, when he was thirteen, Jack was sent to Canterbury School in Milford, Connecticut, the only Catholic school he would ever attend, but he returned home the next spring after an appendicitis attack and missed the remainder of the academic year. In the fall of 1931 he joined

Joe Jr. (left) and John appear to be loving brothers in this 1925 photo. But they were fierce rivals and Joe often bullied John physically.

Joe at Choate, a private prep school whose students were mostly Protestant. Jack was an indifferent scholar but played several sports and was popular even though his thin features won him the nickname "Rat Face." With Kirk LeMoyne Billings, a roommate who became his life-long friend, Jack formed the "Choate Muckers Club." Their pranks, such as throwing food out of dormitory windows, annoyed headmaster Seymour St. John: "They weren't wicked lads, but they were a nuisance. At one time it came to the point where I was saying to myself, 'Well, I have two things to do, one to run the school, another to run Jack Kennedy and his friends.'"[36]

Finally Besting Joe

In June 1935, Jack graduated 64th out of a class of 112. No longer wanting to be overshadowed by Joe, who was attending Harvard, he enrolled in Princeton, where his poor health betrayed him again.

Members of the Choate Muckers Club. From left to right are Ralph Horton, Kirk LeMoyne Billings, Thomas Schriber, and John F. Kennedy.

Jack missed an entire school year with an illness diagnosed as either hepatitis or jaundice, but which may have been an early bout with Addison's disease, an ailment that plagued him as an adult.

After he recuperated, his father persuaded him to attend Harvard, where he again concentrated on sports—football and swimming—and having fun. Gradually, however, Jack turned into a serious student, partly because he became concerned about what was happening in the world after spending several summers in Europe while his father was ambassador to England. He once explained his academic awakening:

> I guess it was during my sophomore year that I really found myself. I don't know what to attribute it to. No. Not professors. I guess I was just getting older. It was during my junior year that I went to England for six months [to work for his father], which meant taking six courses as a senior and hard work.[37]

That work included a senior thesis explaining why England was unprepared for war. His father suggested Jack turn the essay into a book and persuaded *New York Times* journalist Arthur Krock to help Jack improve the manuscript, which became a best-seller when published in 1940 as *Why England Slept*.

Jack had finally overshadowed Joe. He would surpass his brother once more, with dramatic consequences for both brothers.

War Hero

In June 1941 Joe, who had already decided he wanted to become president, enlisted in the navy, partly to protect his future political image by countering his father's increasingly unpopular stance against America's entry into World War II. Jack tried to join the navy after the Japanese attacked Pearl Harbor on December 7, 1941, but he was rejected because of his weak back, ulcers, and asthma. His father wielded his influence in government to get him in despite his poor health. Although Jack was given a job in navy intelligence in Washington, D.C., he wanted to fight in combat, so his father again used his power to have him assigned to command a patrol torpedo (PT) boat in the South Pacific.

Years later when people asked him how he became a war hero, Kennedy would joke, "It was easy—they sank my boat."[38] On the night of August 2, 1943, while his ship was on patrol in the Solomon Islands, the Japanese destroyer *Amagiri* struck PT-109, slicing the small, wooden-hulled boat in half and killing two of Lieutenant Kennedy's thirteen-man crew.

Despite his health problems, Kennedy was a strong swimmer. Towing a sailor who had been badly burned, he led his men on a three-and-a-half-mile swim to nearby Plum Pudding Island. When one man asked, "Will we ever get out of this?" Kennedy responded, "It can be done. We'll do it."[39] Somehow, this pampered young rich man reached deep within himself, finding an inner source of courage to help his men survive the most dangerous, terrifying experience of their lives. Kennedy later led the survivors to another nearby island, Naru, where they encountered friendly natives. With a knife, Kennedy carved these words into a coconut:

John F. Kennedy (left) and his brother, Joe Jr., pose proudly in their navy uniforms.

NATIVE KNOWS POSIT[ION]
HE CAN PILOT 11 ALIVE
NEEDS SMALL BOAT KENNEDY[40]

The natives took the message to Lieutenant Arthur Reginald Evans, an Australian coast watcher who arranged for PT boats to rescue Kennedy's crew on August 8. Kennedy was awarded the Purple Heart as well as the Navy and Marine Corps Medal for bravery in the difficult situation, but in December he was sent home because his back was worse and ulcers and malaria had weakened him, dropping his weight to only 125 pounds on a 6-foot-1-inch frame.

Joe had been flying reconnaissance missions from English bases, but he became so envious of Jack's hero status that he sought a new assignment as the pilot of an experimental bomber. It was dangerous, but Joe wanted to become a hero like Jack. On August 12, 1944, he was killed when his plane blew up in midair. His father, who rarely drank, consumed an entire bottle of scotch when he learned the news and the next day cried for ninety minutes while telling Joe's sisters what happened.

He mourned his oldest son, but did not give up his dream of a president named Kennedy. Joe then decided that his second son would enter politics in place of his brother.

Congressman Kennedy

Jack's war hero status and the power of his last name, still potent in the Kennedys' hometown, made him the leading contender in the 1946 contest for Boston's 11th Congressional District. Kennedy also had the help of his father, who vowed, "We're going to sell Jack like soap flakes."[41] Joe contributed tens of thousands of dollars, hired political experts to run the campaign, and distributed thousands of copies of a magazine article on his son's war exploits. The campaign was a family affair, with Rose and Jack's sisters wooing female voters and Robert and Ted also helping out.

The political neophyte, who would go on to triumph in every election he entered, easily won the Democratic primary. And on November 5, when he crushed Republican Lester W. Bowen 60,093 to just 26,007, John F. "Honey Fitz" Fitzgerald hopped on a table and danced an Irish jig while singing "Sweet Adeline" to celebrate his grandson's victory.

The reluctant candidate was now a reluctant twenty-nine-year-old congressman, one who did not work very hard or do a very good job. This is how Kennedy explained his poor early record: "After all, I wasn't equipped for the job. I didn't plan to get into

A young John F. Kennedy gives a speech during his first campaign for Congress in 1946. He never lost an election for public office.

it, and when I started out as a Congressman, there were lots of things I didn't know, a lot of mistakes I made, maybe some votes that should have been different."[42]

Kennedy was also struggling to escape his dad's influence. "I'd just come out of my father's house and these were the things I knew,"[43] he said of his beliefs. Kennedy tackled working-class issues such as low-cost housing for veterans, but like his father he was conservative on foreign affairs, voting against aid to other countries and criticizing the administration of President Harry S. Truman for not having prevented a Communist takeover in China.

Gradually, however, Kennedy forged his own political identity. After a 1951 fact-finding trip to Europe, he testified at a hearing that America must help foreign nations by giving them financial help. When Kennedy was asked if he no longer agreed with his father, who opposed such aid, he answered, "That is my position. I think you should ask my father directly as to his position."[44]

Private Life

One reason Kennedy was not a great legislator was that he spent more time having fun than working. And like his father, pleasure meant dating a lot of women. In *Seeds of Destruction: Joe Kennedy and His Sons*, Ralph G. Martin writes that when Jack was twelve, he stowed away when his father took actress Gloria Swanson for a sail at Hyannis Port. When Jack saw them kissing he jumped overboard, and Joe had to dive into the water to rescue him. Martin claims this incident in particular, and Joe's womanizing in general, gravely affected the Kennedy brothers:

> For Jack, the impact of what he saw was surely enormous, and lifelong. Besides Gloria, there was a small parade of women, all young all attractive, who arrived at their home at different times with their father. [Jack] and the other sons learned to consider their father's promiscuity as an inherent masculine right.[45]

Jack's good looks, charm, social position, and wealth made it easy for him to date scores of women. But his goal was almost always sexual conquest, not forming a loving relationship with another person.

Kennedy's health problems contributed to his lackadaisical congressional record. In addition to a bad back, ulcers, asthma, and periodic attacks of the malaria he had contracted during the war, Kennedy almost died in 1947 while traveling in Europe to study labor problems. After he was taken home to Boston, doctors diagnosed Addison's disease, which weakens the immune system and makes people susceptible to infectious disease. Kennedy began taking medication to control Addison's, but several times in future years infections would make him critically ill.

Although Kennedy had health problems his entire life, the public believed he was strong and vigorous, the young legislator and president who sailed, played golf, and engaged in fast-paced games of touch football with his brothers and sisters. Biographer Richard Reeves claims the reason for the discrepancy between public perception and private reality is that Jack skillfully concealed his frailties, such as the glasses he wore to read but refused to don in public:

> There was a gallantry to Kennedy's consistent lying about his health and his success in persuading press and public that he was a man of great energy. In truth, boy and man, he was sick and in pain much of the time, often using crutches or a cane in private to rest his back, and taking medication, prescribed and unprescribed, each day, sometimes every hour.[46]

Kennedy's poor health sometimes made him depressed, as did the death of his favorite sister, Kathleen. When she died in an airplane crash in 1948, Jack went into a deep depression that was also fueled by his own illness. Jack's morbid thoughts about death began to influence his personality and he told a friend, "The point is that you've got to live every day like it's your last day on earth. That's what I'm doing."[47]

Senator Kennedy

That attitude was one reason he decided to run for the Senate in 1952 against Republican Henry Cabot Lodge. But Kennedy also hated his lowly status in the House, where he was only one of more than four hundred representatives; he yearned for the recognition and power of a senator. With the help of his family Jack overwhelmed Lodge, a senator since 1936. Joe funded his campaign, Robert managed it, Ted helped out in small ways, and again Rose and her daughters courted women voters. Kennedy biographer James MacGregor Burns describes an elegant tea at the Commander Hotel in Cambridge:

> The star of the affair was Rose Kennedy. Still youthful looking and stylish in a dignified way, she gave a simple motherly tribute to her son that made the real campaign seem far off and somehow unimportant. Sisters Eunice, Jean, and Pat managed the affairs with their usual gusto and charm.[48]

The Kennedy family at their Hyannis Port home in 1948. From left to right are John, Jean, Rose, Joe, Patricia, Robert, and Eunice. Edward is squatting.

Kennedy officially spent $349,646, but it is believed his father secretly contributed several million dollars to a campaign that included telecasts featuring the entire family, an innovation in those early days of television. Years later it was revealed that Joe loaned $500,000 to *Boston Post* owner John Fox so that his newspaper would endorse his son. Jack beat Lodge by more than seventy thousand votes, a victory that was all the sweeter because Lodge's grandfather had defeated "Honey Fitz" for the same seat in 1916.

Jack was sworn in as senator on January 3, 1953, and his life changed again later that year on September 12, when he married Jacqueline Lee Bouvier, a slim, dark-haired beauty who also grew up in a wealthy, prominent family. A dozen years younger than Jack at twenty-four, Jacqueline was the perfect wife for this rising political star: Catholic, intelligent, and beautiful.

Running for President

Kennedy worked harder in the Senate than he had in the House. Before his first term was up in 1958 he led the fight to reform the Electoral College, the constitutional mechanism that dictates how states cast their votes for president, and began investigating labor corruption. While recuperating from back surgery in 1954 he wrote *Profiles in Courage*, a best-seller about U.S. historical figures for which he received the Pulitzer Prize. His ambitions fueled by fears of dying young, he decided to seek the presidency.

At the 1956 Democratic Convention, Jack and Robert waged a last-minute campaign to wrest the presidential nomination from Illinois governor Adlai Stevenson. They were unsuccessful, but Jack vowed to be the Democratic presidential nominee in 1960, and his father was happy to help him. His fortune now swollen to over $400 million, Joe channeled $13 million into Jack's campaign. He also worked quietly to secure endorsements from top politicians and persuade newspapers and magazines to run favorable stories about his son. In his biography of the senior Kennedy, author David E. Koskoff writes, "People in informed circles *knew* the candidate's father was purposefully keeping in the background so that his scandalous past would not come to light."[49]

The 1960 presidential campaign included a tough primary battle with Minnesota senator Hubert H. Humphrey, who claimed so many Kennedys were arrayed against him that "I feel like an independent merchant competing against a chain store."[50] Robert was Jack's campaign manager, Ted headed up activities in western states, and Jacqueline, Rose, and other family members campaigned across the nation.

John F. Kennedy and his bride, Jacqueline Bouvier, cut their wedding cake after being married September 12, 1953.

Kennedy's biggest challenge was to overcome religious prejudice; some people feared that a Catholic president could be improperly influenced by church officials. He defused this thorny issue in the West Virginia primary with a dramatic televised speech in which he explained that the U.S. Constitution's strict separation of church and state made that impossible. He defeated Humphrey in West Virginia and went on to win the Democratic nomination.

In the general election, Kennedy had to prove he was as competent and experienced as Republican Richard Nixon, a former congressman who was vice president for eight years under President Dwight D. Eisenhower. Many historians believe the campaign's turning point was the election's first televised debate on September 26, in which Kennedy came across as more articulate, knowledgeable, and attractive than Nixon. In *The Making of the President 1960*, Theodore H. White writes:

> Kennedy was calm and nerveless in appearance. The vice president, by contrast, was tense, almost frightened, at turns glowering and, occasionally, haggard-looking to the point of sickness. . . . After the debates there was a quantum jump in the size of Kennedy crowds [at political rallies].[51]

Kennedy defeated Nixon by only 114,673 votes out of more than 68 million cast, but in the Electoral College he won 303 to 219. At age forty-three, he was the youngest president ever elected.

The Cuban Missile Crisis

His presidency began on a high note with his inspiring inaugural speech, but within a few months the Kennedy administration became mired in controversy when Cuban exiles unsuccessfully invaded the nearby island nation in an attempt to overthrow the communist regime of dictator Fidel Castro. The so-called Bay of Pigs military operation in April 1961 was planned by the Eisenhower administration but Kennedy had to give it his final approval, and he was criticized for its failure when Castro's army easily defeated the poorly organized invaders.

Kennedy granted his permission for the operation because military advisers told him it could not fail, but he later realized he should never have trusted their advice for such an important decision. "All my life I've known better than to depend on the experts. How could I have been so stupid, to let them [the exiles] go ahead?"[52] said Kennedy, who normally based his actions on his own knowledge and instincts. A little more than a year later, this small island nation would again bedevil him during the Cuban Missile Crisis.

John F. Kennedy and his Republican opponent, Richard M. Nixon, shake hands after their televised debate on October 7, 1960.

On October 16, 1962, photographs taken by a spy plane high over Cuba showed that Soviet technicians were building facilities that could launch nuclear missiles against the United States. Because of the failed invasion earlier, Soviet premier Nikita Khrushchev believed Kennedy was weak and would not do anything about the missile threat. But Khrushchev was wrong. Kennedy was ready, declaring, "I guess this is the week I earn my salary."[53]

In a televised speech October 22, Kennedy demanded removal of the missiles and ordered a naval blockade to stop further military shipments to Cuba. He said the drastic measure had to be taken because building the missile site was "a deliberate provocation and unjustified change in status quo [in the area] which cannot be accepted by this country, if our courage and our commitments are ever to be trusted by either friend or foe."[54] It was a bold move, one that many feared might ignite nuclear war with the Soviet Union, but after a few tense days the Soviets agreed to remove the missiles.

Civil Rights

The nation had survived one of its most serious political crises and the young president had gained great prestige for having stood up to Khrushchev, but Cuba was only one of many problems Kennedy dealt with at home and abroad. One of the most difficult was the growing division in America over civil rights.

Kennedy and his brother, Robert, whom he appointed attorney general, supported African Americans in their fight against racist laws that segregated them and denied them basic rights. As violence repeatedly broke out in southern states when African Americans enrolled in white-only public schools and marched to protest other injustices, Kennedy decided it was time for the federal government to act.

The president ordered federal officials to take a more active role in fighting racist policies and began proposing legislation to protect civil rights. On June 11, 1963, Kennedy declared in a televised speech that America must be dedicated to "the proposal that race has no place in American life or law."[55] He announced a civil rights bill that would ban discrimination in public accommodations, such as hotels and restaurants, and forbid discrimination in any state program receiving federal aid, such as schools, welfare, and highway construction. The bill gave the federal government power to force desegregation of public schools, something that was not being done in most areas of the nation despite the 1954 U.S. Supreme Court decision *Brown v. Board of Education*, which had declared segregated schools illegal.

Both provisions were major breakthroughs for African Americans. The bill would not be passed until after his death, but at least Kennedy made a start in correcting a moral problem he said was "as old as the Scriptures and [as] clear as the American Constitution."[56]

Other Achievements

One of Kennedy's biggest strengths was his ability to inspire people, and this power was never greater than in 1961 when he promised to conquer space by landing men on the moon within a decade. "We set sail on this new sea," Kennedy would later say, "because there is new knowledge to be gained, and new rights to be won, and they must be won and used for the progress of all people."[57] His daring challenge made Americans believe they could do something that seemed impossible; on July 29, 1969, Neil Armstrong set foot on the moon to fulfill Kennedy's startling timetable.

The most difficult foreign problem was America's hostile relationship with the Soviet Union. Instead of gloating over his victory after the missile crisis, Kennedy started working to ease tensions with the Soviets. One of his greatest triumphs came on October 7, 1963, when he signed a Limited Nuclear Test Ban Treaty in which both nations agreed to decrease such tests, which were polluting the environment with radiation. Kennedy proposed the ban and persuaded the Soviets to accept it.

Kennedy also created the Alliance for Progress to help developing nations in Latin America, and the Peace Corps, but he had his share of defeats. His proposals to subsidize medical care for the elderly—a program that was later enacted and is known today as Medicare—and to lower taxes were both rejected by Congress, which also stalled his civil rights bill.

Despite the difficulties of the office, Kennedy decided to seek a second term. It was to build support for his campaign that he traveled to Dallas, Texas, in November 1963.

Death of a President

As Kennedy rode through Dallas on November 22, a huge crowd cheering his open-aired limousine as his motorcade passed, the nation's thirty-fifth president was shot by an assassin. Jacqueline, seated next to him, reacted in shock: "My God, what are they doing? My God, they've killed Jack. They've killed my husband."[58] The presidential limousine sped to a nearby hospital, where Kennedy, who had been shot three times including once in the head, was pronounced dead.

It was determined that the shots had come from the nearby Texas School Book Depository. Shortly after police entered the

President John F. Kennedy waves to people lining the route of his motorcade in Dallas on November 22, 1963.

building, a worker named Lee Harvey Oswald was seen fleeing. On the sixth floor, officers found the rifle that had fired the shots, a World War II Italian-made Mannlicher-Carcano. Oswald was arrested a few hours later, but he was never brought to trial. Two days later while he was being transferred to another jail, Oswald himself was shot to death by nightclub operator Jack Ruby.

Unfulfilled Promise

The assassination meant that the world would never know what this young president might have accomplished had he lived and been reelected. Theodore Sorensen, one of Kennedy's top aides, claims that "with all his accomplishments in the past, he seemed to be destined to accomplish still more in the future."[59]

It is debated even today whether Kennedy would have fully committed America to the Vietnam War, a conflict that proved disastrous for the nation. Even though Kennedy sent several thousand soldiers to Vietnam, there were indications that he believed it would be impossible to win such a war and was preparing to bring most of them home if he was reelected. It was his successor, Vice President Lyndon B. Johnson, who escalated U.S. involvement in Vietnam. Historians also debate whether Kennedy might have been able to help ease racial problems that worsened in the next decade or foster friendlier relations with the Soviet Union.

But because of an assassin's bullet, the world would never know what might have been. As James Reston of the *New York Times* wrote, "What was killed was not only the President but the promise."[60]

CHAPTER 3

Robert Francis Kennedy: The Third Son

The slaying of his older brother was a mortal blow to Robert Francis Kennedy. In his biography of the family's third-born son, Ralph de Toledano writes:

> The man to suffer least from the assassin's bullet was President [John F.] Kennedy. The man who suffered most was Robert Kennedy. In every conceivable way, he was grievously wounded, perhaps irreparably so. For Bobby Kennedy's adult existence had been a function of his brother Jack's life.[61]

With stunning, horrifying swiftness, Bobby had become the family's oldest surviving son. He would now have to follow a path that Jack had predicted years earlier his brother would take if anything ever happened to him. While recovering from back surgery in 1954, his own mortality weighing heavily on his mind, Jack made a statement that sounded as if it were coming from a member of royalty talking about the right of succession to a family title: "Just as I went into politics when Joe died, if anything happened to me tomorrow, my brother Bobby would run for my seat. And if anything happened to him, my brother Teddy would run."[62]

Bobby, whom his father had always referred to as the "runt" of the family, became the third son to inherit the Kennedy mantle of political leadership.

Growing Up in the Shadows

By the time he was born November 20, 1925, the seventh child, a family hierarchy had emerged with Joe, Jack, and Kathleen composing an elite trio. The older Kennedys were good-looking, confident, and intelligent and, as a family friend once remarked, "They were the pick of the litter, the ones the old man thought could write the story of the next generation."[63]

Smaller, less gifted athletically and academically, more timid and shy than his brothers, Bobby had trouble securing his own place in

Robert Kennedy (middle) is flanked by brothers John (left) and Edward in this picture taken in the 1940s at Hyannis Port.

this highly competitive family. But he won Rose's praise for being her most religious child, one who assisted priests during mass at St. Joseph's Catholic Church in Bronxville, New York: "Bobby has taken his religion seriously,"[64] she said. His religious zeal would give him a stiff, unbending sense of morality his entire life.

Bobby's childhood was unsettling because the family continually moved, from Brookline, Massachusetts, to Bronxville and then to London, England. First sent to boarding school when he was seven, he once commented:

> What I remember most vividly about growing up was going to a lot of different schools, always having to make new friends, and that I was very awkward. I dropped things and fell down all the time. I had to go to the hospital a few times for stitches in my head and my legs. And I was pretty quiet most of the time. And I didn't mind being alone.[65]

The Kennedys moved back to the United States in 1940 and Bobby went to Portsmouth (Rhode Island) Abbey Priory. He struggled with his studies: His marks were in the 60s and 70s on a scale of 100 and he was caught cheating on an English exam. It was unusual for a Kennedy to have academic problems, which he acknowledged in a letter to his father: "I don't know where I get my brains. But it's quite evident that I received them from neither my father nor my mother."[66]

His difficulty in matching the accomplishments of his siblings helped the "runt" develop a tenacity, hardness, and pugnacity that toughened him. "I was the seventh of nine children," Kennedy once said, "and when you come from that far down you have to struggle to survive."[67]

The Navy and Harvard

In 1942 Kennedy entered Milton Academy, a prep school south of Boston favored by children from rich Protestant families, and after graduation went into the navy against his father's wishes. Kennedy began attending officer's school at Harvard, but in the fall of 1945 he quit so he could become an enlisted man on a destroyer that had been christened the *Joseph P. Kennedy Jr.* in honor of his late brother.

In early 1946 the apprentice seaman reported to the *Kennedy*, where he chipped paint, performed other routine jobs, and for the first time lived with young men from more humble circumstances. "I certainly am meeting people with a different outlook & interests in life,"[68] he wrote his parents.

Kennedy returned to Harvard needing only three more semesters to graduate because of credits he earned during his naval studies. A mediocre student, Kennedy was put on probation for poor grades in the winter of 1946–1947, but he managed one success neither of his brothers had, lettering in football like their father. To earn his crimson "H," Kennedy had to make up for his lack of athletic ability and size (he was five feet ten inches and weighed 150 pounds) with grit and determination. He won his letter for playing briefly against Yale despite a fractured leg, which was protected by a heavy cast. Said Kenny O'Donnell, who was team captain and became his lifelong friend: "I can't think of anyone who had less right to make the varsity squad than Bobby when he first came out for practice. But every afternoon he would be down on the field an hour early, and he always stayed an hour later. He just made himself better."[69]

Law School and Marriage

Kennedy spent several months abroad after graduating in 1948 and briefly tried journalism, writing articles for the *Boston Post* on a variety of topics. Despite his mediocre grades, his father's influence won him acceptance that fall at the University of Virginia Law School.

Driving an old Chrysler convertible and living in a small house close to railroad tracks, Kennedy studied hard and went to church daily. Kennedy did not date many girls but he found a companion for life in Ethel Skakel, a roommate of his sister, Jean, at Manhattanville College of the Sacred Heart in Purchase, New York. Ethel was also from a wealthy Catholic family and very religious, but more vivacious and outgoing than Robert. Her college yearbook described her this way: "An excited hoarse voice, a shriek, a peal of screaming laughter, the flash of shirttails, a tousled brown head—Ethel! Her face is at one moment a picture of utter guilelessness and at the next alive with mischief."[70]

They were married in 1950. When Kennedy graduated in June 1951, 56th in a class of 124, he became a U.S. Department of Justice lawyer in New York City. But a higher priority soon made him give up the job—helping Jack win a campaign.

Electing Jack

Bobby had worked hard in Jack's first congressional race, but it was in his 1952 Senate bid that he became one of his brother's most formidable political weapons. Jack asked him to run the campaign and he took command with a ruthless manner that left no doubt about who was in charge. Bobby was efficient but often abrasive personally: "I don't care if anyone around here likes me, as long as they like Jack."[71]

Robert Kennedy and his wife, Ethel, whom he married in 1950.

Senator Joseph McCarthy and Robert Kennedy at the White House. Kennedy worked briefly for the controversial senator, but eventually quit.

He directed all the facets of the statewide campaign and once had to speak in support of his brother when no other Kennedy was available. It was one of the shortest political speeches ever given:

> My brother Jack couldn't be here, my mother couldn't be here, my sister Eunice couldn't be here, my sister Pat couldn't be here, my sister Jean couldn't be here, but if my brother Jack were here, he'd tell you [Henry Cabot] Lodge has a very bad voting record. Thank you.[72]

Government Lawyer

After helping his brother win the election, Kennedy was hired in January 1953 as a lawyer on the Senate Permanent Subcommittee on Investigations chaired by Senator Joseph McCarthy, a friend of his father's. The Wisconsin Republican became infamous for his unscrupulous hunt for Communists, a campaign in which he made false charges against hundreds of innocent people just to support his witch hunt. Like many people, Kennedy at first defended McCarthy's tactics, saying, "His methods may be a little too rough. But after all, his goal is to expose Communists in government."[73] However, Kennedy quit his job six months later when he began to realize that what McCarthy was doing was wrong.

Kennedy returned as chief counsel the following year when Arkansas Democrat John McClellan became chair of the powerful subcommittee. The post would vault Kennedy to national prominence in 1957 when he began investigating corruption in labor and organized crime. His main target was the Teamsters Union, which represented truck drivers. Much of the testimony in the hearings before the Labor Rackets Committee was dramatic, as when Kennedy questioned Joseph "Joey" Glimco, president of the Teamsters' Chicago local:

> KENNEDY: And you defraud the union?
> GLIMCO: I respectfully decline to answer because I honestly believe my answer might tend to incriminate me.
> KENNEDY: I would agree with you. You haven't got the guts to answer, have you, Mr. Glimco?[74]

Some people criticized Kennedy for treating witnesses too harshly, but his tough demeanor made him popular with many Americans. Teamsters president Dave Beck was found guilty of illegally using union funds and was succeeded by James Hoffa, who himself was suspected of racketeering. Kennedy tried unsuccessfully for several years to convict Hoffa and they grew to hate each other, with Hoffa labeling him "a spoiled young millionaire that never had to go out and find a way to live by his own efforts."[75] Kennedy and his staff eventually collected the evidence that sent the labor leader to prison in 1967 on charges of jury tampering, fraud, and conspiracy.

Jack and Robert

Jack was a member of the Labor Rackets Committee, and the televised hearings paired the brothers in the public's mind for the first time. Because they had never been close while growing up, Jack did not learn to appreciate Bobby until they were adults. Arthur M. Schlesinger, an aide to President Kennedy who authored biographies of both brothers, claims they grew closer when Bobby accompanied Jack on a 1951 fact-finding journey to Israel and Japan:

> The trip in a real sense introduced Robert Kennedy to his older brother. "The first time I remember meeting Bobby," Jack once said, "was when he was three and a half, one summer on the Cape [Cod]." Soon John left home, for school, for college, for war. Afterward Robert was away at college and law school. Seven weeks of arduous travel made them closer than ever before.[76]

Jack began to respect his brother's intellect and personality, which was more pragmatic and tougher than his own, and Bobby became more determined to help Jack succeed. Their relationship was also strengthened when Bobby managed Jack's 1952 Senate campaign and, according to biographer Evan Thomas, began to watch out for his older sibling's best interests: "RFK had always protected his brother's secrets, from the time he hid JFK's crutches in the car during the 1952 Massachusetts Senate campaign."[77] Jack's back was so painful that he often used crutches to walk, but public knowledge of the infirmity could have doomed his campaign.

Bobby helped Jack win reelection in 1958 and then headed his 1960 bid for the presidency. He again ran the campaign with military precision but not much diplomacy. Victor Lasky's *JFK: The Man and the Myth*, written before Jack's assassination, was the first book to criticize the Kennedys for the ruthless way they sought power and wealth. In the book, Lasky commented on Bobby:

> As his brother's campaign manager, Bobby Kennedy offended almost everyone with whom he came into contact. His attitude was perhaps best summed up in the remark he made to [New York Democrats]. "Gentlemen, I don't give a damn if the state and city organizations survive after November, and I don't give a damn if *you* survive. I want to elect John F. Kennedy."[78]

But his hard-bitten attitude worked. Jack was elected, and Bobby became attorney general.

His Brother's Confidante

Jack assembled a group of talented cabinet officials who would be collectively nicknamed "the Best and Brightest," including Defense Secretary Robert McNamara and Secretary of State Dean Rusk. Even though he risked charges of nepotism, Jack named Bobby to head the Justice Department. Fearing a controversy over his selection would hurt his brother, Bobby at first refused, relenting only after Jack explained why he needed him: "In this cabinet, there really is no person with whom I have been intimately connected over the years. I need to know that when problems arise I'm going to have somebody who's going to tell me the unvarnished truth, no matter what . . . and [you] will do that."[79]

Kennedy was a strong, capable attorney general, but it was as an adviser that he did his greatest service to his brother and his country. He was never more valuable than during the Cuban Missile Crisis. After discovering on October 16, 1962, that the Soviet

Union was building a nuclear missile site in Cuba, the president named twenty-one officials to the Executive Committee of the National Security Council (ExComm) to help him decide how to respond to the crisis. He personally chose Bobby to chair this important group. ExComm members considered several options, including direct military action, but Bobby opposed that choice:

> I could not accept the idea that the United States would rain bombs on Cuba, killing thousands of civilians in a surprise attack. Each of us was being asked to make a recommendation which, if wrong and if accepted, could mean the destruction of the human race [in a nuclear war with the Soviet Union].[80]

ExComm decided on a naval blockade that would cut off shipments to Cuba until the missile sites were dismantled. After announcing the action October 22, U.S. officials waited nervously to see whether Soviet ships bound for Cuba would honor the blockade. The crisis eased on October 24 when a half-dozen vessels stopped short of the military line formed by U.S. ships.

Two days later, Soviet premier Nikita Khrushchev sent a letter agreeing to remove the missiles in return for a U.S. pledge not to invade Cuba. Before the president could respond, however, the Soviet leader sent a second note, now saying he would take them out *only* if America did the same with missiles it had in Turkey. The conflicting offers confused ExComm members, who became di-

Robert Kennedy and his brother John during a Senate hearing into organized crime.

vided on how to respond. But Bobby came up with a brilliant suggestion: "Ignore the second letter and answer the first."[81]

The president sent a letter agreeing to the first proposal and threatening to bomb Cuba if the offer was not made good. The Soviets accepted the offer to end the crisis.

Civil Rights

Although Kennedy played an important role as a personal adviser to his brother on matters such as the Cuban Missile Crisis, his official role in the Kennedy administration was as attorney general, where he continued to probe labor corruption and organized crime. But a more serious, urgent problem soon began to demand his attention—the fight by African Americans against racism. Although the Kennedys supported the civil rights cause, they wanted to move more cautiously than African Americans. In *Remembering Kennedy: One Brief Shining Moment*, William Manchester comments on this conflict:

> Bobby in his first speech as Attorney General in Athens, Georgia, on May 6, 1961 said if blacks were not treated equally "the Department of Justice will act. We will not stand by or be aloof." Of course, as he and his brother had privately explained to black leaders, these things took *time*. They couldn't expect it all *now*. That was the flaw: the blacks wanted it now.[82]

The Kennedys were worried that helping African Americans would alienate white southern voters, dooming Jack's chance of re-election in 1964. But as civil rights protests in the South were met with appalling violence and the brothers learned more about how bad discrimination was, they began to act more forcibly. They ordered federal marshals to protect students enrolling in all-white colleges, hired more African American employees, and put the power of the government firmly behind the drive for civil rights.

Biographer Ralph G. Martin claims Bobby, at first tentative in supporting this historic fight, eventually "became the presidential prod on civil rights issues."[83] Bobby goaded Jack to do more for African Americans and influenced him on June 22, 1963, to introduce the Civil Rights Act, which banned segregation in public facilities. Congress would pass the bill, but only after Jack's assassination; the 1964 Civil Rights Act would be signed into law by Lyndon Johnson.

On November 22, 1963, the day his brother was killed in Dallas, Kennedy was meeting with Justice Department officials at

Robert F. Kennedy addresses a crowd during a civil rights demonstration on June 14, 1963, in Washington, D.C.

Hickory Hill, the six-and-a-half acre estate in McLean, Virginia, he had bought from Jack. As biographer Ralph de Toledano explains, Kennedy liked working at home to be near his wife and eight children (three more children would be born to the Kennedys, one after Bobby's assassination):

> No matter how full his schedule, Bobby tries to be home for dinner and plunges into the family life with zest, catching up on what the children have been doing, what their concerns are. When it is bedtime, the Kennedys supervise the nightly prayers of the children—the traditional "Now I lay me down to sleep," and a short verse asking the angel of God to watch over them.[84]

At 1:45 P.M. while he was munching on a tuna fish sandwich, Kennedy received a telephone call from Federal Bureau of Investigation director J. Edgar Hoover, who told him his brother had been shot. Stunned, Kennedy told Ethel and then, as other telephones began ringing, he wandered from one to another answering them. Between calls he muttered, "I thought they'd get one of us. I thought it would be me."[85] The brothers had made many enemies, and Robert had been more hated than Jack because of his abrasive personality.

The death was an ordeal for Bobby. Although he overcame his own sadness only after weeks of brooding and sorrow, Kirk

LeMoyne Billings said Bobby helped other Kennedys deal with their grief: "The whole family was like a bunch of shipwreck survivors. I don't think they could have made it all without Bobby. He always had an arm around a friend or family member and was telling them it was okay, that it was time to move ahead."[86]

Kennedy, too, had to move ahead. He did not like President Lyndon B. Johnson, so he resigned as attorney general on September 2, 1964, to run for a New York Senate seat. Nicholas Katzenbach, his deputy attorney general, said Kennedy understood he had to take over for his slain brother: "I don't think Bob had any great sense of dynasty, but when Jack died Bob felt he had a responsibility to carry on what Jack had started."[87] Kennedy beat Kenneth Keating on November 3 by 700,000 votes.

Bobby was not a charismatic campaigner like Jack, yet many people supported him just because he was a Kennedy. In his biography of the brothers, Richard D. Mahoney writes that Kennedy struggled to deal with his brother's legacy:

Robert and Ethel Kennedy had a large family. His eleventh child was born after his assassination.

The problem for Bobby was that he wanted to be Jack, and wasn't. When people saw him in person or on television, they wanted the same thing—Jack—but instead they saw a small man, possibly unhappy, definitely uneasy, and not nearly as good-looking. . . . When he drew loud crowds in the Senate campaign in 1964, he said, "Don't you know? They're for him. They're for him."[88]

Senator Kennedy

Sworn in with his brother, Ted, who was reelected to Jack's old seat, Kennedy quickly established himself as one of the Senate's most influential members, a critic of Johnson and chief spokesman for liberal Democrats. Although Kennedy could be tough and uncaring at times, the morality stemming from his religious beliefs began to make him more compassionate.

Historian Lester David writes that Robert in many ways had been as conservative as his father until "the last seven years of his life when his eyes were opened to the poverty of those who had been bypassed by social and economic progress."[89] Part of that awakening came during a fact-finding trip to Mississippi in April 1967, when he was enraged by the dismal living conditions of African American workers. "My god," said Kennedy, " I didn't know this kind of thing existed. How can a country like this allow it?"[90]

Kennedy attacked Johnson for escalating U.S. involvement in the Vietnam War, claiming the fighting was killing innocent civilians. As the country became bitterly divided over the war, Kennedy wanted to run against Johnson in 1968, but hung back because he feared his candidacy would hurt the Democratic Party. Others believed he was afraid of Johnson. His detractors taunted him, waving signs when he appeared in public that read "Kennedy: Hawk, Dove—or Chicken." (A hawk was someone who favored U.S. participation in the war, a dove someone who wanted to end that involvement.)

Minnesota senator Eugene McCarthy ran for the Democratic nomination on an antiwar platform. When he upset Johnson in the New Hampshire primary on March 12, 1968, Kennedy decided to challenge Johnson too, and entered the race on March 16. Although some still criticized him for not having had the courage to face Johnson until McCarthy did, Kennedy's campaign became successful. He received 52 percent of the vote to win Indiana, the first primary he entered, and by June 4 had captured five out of six primary elections.

Kennedy's candidacy galvanized thousands of housewives, farmers, workers, and college students, who flocked to his rallies bearing signs reading "I Love You, Bobby" or "Bobby is Groovy." Near the end of his eighty-one-day campaign, Kennedy remarked to Kenny O'Donnell, "You know, I feel now for the first time that I've shaken off the shadow of my brother. I feel I made it on my own."[91]

Another Bullet

His final victory was in the June 4 California primary. At one minute after midnight June 5, he left his suite at the Embassy Hotel in Los Angeles to address his supporters. After telling them he could win the presidency and unite the nation, Kennedy made his way to a news conference through a kitchen area to bypass large crowds in other areas of the hotel.

At 12:16 A.M., with pro football player Rosie Grier, Olympic decathlon champion Rafer Johnson, and others escorting Kennedy, Sirhan Bishara Sirhan, a Palestinian immigrant, stepped forward and fired eight shots. Bobby was hit three times, including once in the head, a wound similar to the one Jack had suffered. While cries of, "Oh, God! It can't be! Not Again!" filled the air, Ethel, bent over her husband, screamed "Give him air! Air!"[92]

He was declared dead at 1:44 A.M., another Kennedy fallen to an assassin's bullet. For two days, tens of thousands of people filed past his casket in St. Patrick's Cathedral in New York, the line of mourners at times stretching twenty-five blocks long outside the church despite wilting summer heat. On June 7 he was buried next to his brother in Arlington National Cemetery.

More Promise Unfulfilled

In his eulogy at Bobby's funeral, Ted noted, "My brother need not be idealized or enlarged in death beyond what he was in life."[93] Robert Francis Kennedy had accomplished many great things before he was killed; as a Senate investigator he battled corruption in labor and organized crime, as attorney general he helped place the power of the federal government squarely behind the fight for civil rights, and as a confidant to his brother, he helped guide the nation through the Cuban Missile Crisis.

Claiming that it was an ability to envision a better future for America that enabled his brother to do so much for his country, Ted loosely paraphrased a quotation by playwright George Bernard Shaw to explain Bobby's attitude toward life: "Some men see things as they are and say, 'Why?' I dream of things that never were and say, 'Why not?'"[94] And millions of Americans were left to ponder, once again, the question: "Why did a Kennedy have to die?"

CHAPTER 4

Edward Moore "Ted" Kennedy: The Last Son

Joseph P. Kennedy was delighted when his son John was elected president, but he actually held an even more grandiose vision of his family's future. He once told a friend that he believed that Robert and Edward would also one day hold the nation's highest office:

> Each of those three kids is going to be president of the United States. There would have been four if Joe had lived. That's three presidents named Kennedy going down in the history books, one after the other. [Joe then gave a small laugh, adding that] Three Kennedys beat two Adamses.[95]

As arrogant as the elder Kennedy's boast sounds today, many Americans following John's assassination believed it was only natural that Robert and Edward would pursue the position their brother had held; it was a national expectation their father had worked hard most of his life to create. In royal families, titles such as duke and earl are passed on to the oldest surviving sons. In the same way, many Americans believed that it was only fitting that the oldest surviving Kennedy run for president.

Yet only one son would fulfill their father's audacious prediction. It was Sirhan Bishara Sirhan who brutally kept Robert from pursuing the White House, but Ted's presidential dream would die an even uglier death. This time, however, the mortal wounds would be self-inflicted by the Kennedy known as "the last son."

Youth

Born February 22, 1932, the Kennedy's ninth and final child was named Edward Moore Kennedy over the objections of John, who had recommended "George Washington Kennedy." Instead of being christened after the nation's first president, with whom he shared a birthday, the infant was named after Edward Moore, Joe's confidential secretary and closest friend. Just as John would always be known to the family as Jack, Edward became "Teddy" and later "Ted." When Ted was born, John, who was fourteen and attending Choate, wrote his mother to ask, "Can I be Godfather to the baby?"[96] Decades later, Ted would proudly display the letter in his Senate office.

The newest Kennedy was a happy baby who grew into an amiable, chubby youngster, one who sometimes signed letters "fat Ted" and was doted on by his parents. "I admit," Rose once said, "that with Teddy, I did things a little different than I did with the other children. He was my baby, and I tried to keep him that way."[97] Joe, usually a gruff, demanding father, called this happy little boy "sunshine" because Teddy could make him smile.

When the Kennedys moved to England after their father was named U.S. ambassador, the news media began treating family members as celebrities. Photographers took pictures of the Kennedy children and chronicled their adventures in London and visits to other parts of Europe. Seven-year-old Ted held his first news conference in March 1939 after the Kennedys, devout Catholics, met privately with Pope Pius XII, the leader of the Roman Catholic Church. The youngster told a group of reporters how he climbed up on the pope's knee: "I told my sister Patricia I wasn't frightened at all. The pope patted my head and told me I was a smart little fellow."[98]

Unhappiness, Too

Ted, however, was not always a happy, confident child. For one thing, he had trouble competing with siblings who all seemed

The Kennedy family outside the Vatican in Rome before meeting Pope Pius XII in 1939.

smarter and more athletic. Even though Ted developed a strong bond of affection for Joe, his oldest brother once threw the seven-year-old overboard during a sailboat race because he failed to carry out a task. "I was scared to death practically," Kennedy remembered. "I then felt his hands grab my shirt and he lifted me into the boat. We continued the race, and came in second. He got very, very mad."[99]

The youngest Kennedy was also unhappy because he was shifted around so much. By the time he was thirteen, Ted had attended ten different schools, a situation biographer Doris Kearns Goodwin believes hurt him: "For any child, this constant transplantation would be hard. For young Teddy, unsure of his intellect and so overweight at the time that his brothers called him 'fatstuff,' it was extremely damaging."[100]

After the family returned from England, Rose sent Ted to Portsmouth (Rhode Island) Abbey Priory, Bobby's school. Ted, however, was only eight years old, too young for the school's lowest grade, and after three months he was sent home. He attended Riverdale (New York) School for Boys but finished the fourth grade in Palm Beach (Florida) Private School after he became sick with pneumonia and whooping cough. At both new schools he lived at home, which made him happier.

Sports were a big part of Kennedy family life. Left to right in this 1941 photo are Eunice, Robert, Edward, and Jean after playing tennis in Palm Beach, Florida.

The two youngest boys were close, but Bobby could be tough on his little brother. At the Priory, Bobby once walked past Teddy while an older boy was beating him. Teddy asked for help, but Bobby said, "You're a Kennedy . . . take care of yourself."[101] Bobby, however, helped Ted more than any other sibling, calling him at whatever school he was attending, visiting him, and spending holidays with him when other family members were absent. Remembers Ted:

> On the two or three weekends I was able to get away from school, if I couldn't get home, he'd spend the weekend with me. I'll never forget how we used to go to the big empty house at Cape Cod—just the two of us rattling around alone. But Bobby was in charge, taking care of me and making sure I had something to do.[102]

A Big Mistake

Ted's longest stay in one school was four years at Milton Academy, where he began the ninth grade in 1946. Although a mediocre student, he blossomed there physically, growing taller, shedding his baby fat, and becoming confident because he was a good athlete. He graduated in 1950 with a C average, which was good enough, thanks to family influence, to win acceptance to Harvard like his brothers.

As had Bobby, Ted earned Rose's approval by becoming a "religious policeman," waking his roommates at 7 A.M. so they would not miss mass during Lent, the holy time for Catholics before Easter. Despite the display of piety Ted, like his brothers, concentrated more on having fun and playing football than studying. At six feet two inches and a solid two hundred pounds, Ted was more suited for the family's favorite sport than his brothers and made the freshman squad.

His love for football, however, got him into trouble. At the end of his first year in college, Kennedy was so worried that a low grade in Spanish would make him ineligible to play next season that he paid another student to take an important test. He was caught and expelled from school, but Harvard said he could return after a year if he could show he was a responsible citizen. Joe reacted angrily to his son's mistake. "He went absolutely wild and then went up through the roof for about five hours,"[103] Kennedy recalled.

To prove he was a good citizen, Kennedy enlisted in the army, with his father making sure he was stationed in Europe, far from the horror of the Korean War raging on the other side of the world. His army duty was easy and he had time to climb mountains and engage in other daredevil pursuits such as bobsled racing, but biographer Joe McGinniss believes being an enlisted man was good for Ted:

> [It] exposed him first hand to the fact that many people, especially blacks, came from severely disadvantaged backgrounds, and that so much of what he had taken for granted all his life was utterly foreign to them and, moreover, forever unobtainable by them. Upon his return, he quietly began to set aside some time each week to travel to a section of Boston's predominantly black and Puerto Rican South End to work as a basketball coach with underprivileged youths.[104]

"Cadillac Eddie"

Ted returned to Harvard in 1953. He was only an average student but by far the best Kennedy at football, and he made his father proud by catching a seven-yard touchdown pass against Yale on November 19, 1955, before a crowd of more than fifty thousand. He graduated in 1956 and followed Bobby to the University of Virginia Law School, where he and John Tunney, son of former heavyweight boxing champion Gene Tunney, rented a house off campus.

Like Bobby, Ted was not a great student. But unlike his older, more straitlaced brother, he earned the nickname "Cadillac Eddie" for his fun-loving lifestyle. Ted dated a lot of women and was cited several times for speeding and reckless driving, leading Bobby to joke, "My mother wants to know on what side of the court my brother is going to appear when he gets out of law school, attorney or defendant."[105] Unlike other Kennedys who drank moderately, if at all, Ted consumed a lot of alcohol, which contributed to his wildness.

In his second year in law school, Kennedy met Joan Bennett during a visit to the Manhattanville College of the Sacred Heart in Purchase, New York. Filling in for Jack, he was there to dedicate a gymnasium the Kennedys had funded for the school his mother and sisters Eunice and Jean had attended. The couple fell in love, and even Rose, usually critical of women her sons dated, approved of the blond, beautiful Joan, whose family was also rich, Catholic, and had once lived in Bronxville, New York, near the Kennedys.

They were wed November 29, 1958, at St. Joseph's Roman Catholic Church in Bronxville, by Francis Cardinal Spellman. The couple had wanted a priest who was a friend to perform the ceremony, but Joe overruled them, saying the family was so important that a cardinal had to officiate. Jack was Ted's best man. After graduating from law school the next spring, Ted would help elect him president.

Helping Jack

While stationed in Europe, Ted had convinced eight Massachusetts soldiers to cast absentee ballots for Jack's 1952 Senate race. And in 1960 he worked full-time in Jack's presidential campaign, taking command of the vote-getting effort in thirteen western states.

Like his brothers, Ted enjoyed adventure, and during the campaign he performed several dangerous stunts to win votes. The first came in early 1960 during the Wisconsin Democratic primary, when he was told that before he could speak at a ski meet, he had to go down a ski jump, something he had never done. Ted completed the terrifying stunt and in June he rode a bucking bronco in Miles City, Montana, in another attempt to impress voters. Ted explained why he roared down the ski jump even though it frightened him: "I wanted to get off the jump, but if I did, I was afraid my brother would hear of it, and if he heard of it, I would be back in Washington licking stamps and addressing envelopes for the rest of the campaign."[106]

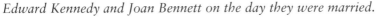

Edward Kennedy and Joan Bennett on the day they were married.

Even though ten of his thirteen states failed to support Jack in the general election, Ted had worked hard. And Ted, like Bobby, was rewarded when Jack became president.

Rewarding Teddy

The youngest Kennedy had always felt overshadowed by his older brothers. After the campaign, he decided to move west and make a new life for himself so far from his siblings that he would never be compared to them again. But his father had other plans. Joe refused to allow Ted to move and then ordered his other two sons to help him win the Senate seat Jack surrendered to become president. "You boys have what you want now, and everyone else helped you work to get it," he said. "Now, it's Ted's turn. Whatever he wants, I'm going to see he gets it."[107]

Jack was concerned that Ted's election would add fuel to growing public resentment over the power the Kennedys were accumulating. Forced into politics himself when his brother Joe died, Jack also believed that one Kennedy should be allowed to lead a more carefree life. "We ought to have one playboy in the family," Jack told Joe, "and that's Ted. Don't force him into politics. Let him be the playboy."[108] With the Kennedy millions, Ted could have spent a lifetime seeking pleasure, but what his sons wanted did not matter to Joe. Bobby admitted years later: "The person who was primarily interested in having him run was my father. Just as I would never have been attorney general if it hadn't been for him."[109]

One problem was that at twenty-eight, Ted was not old enough to be a senator. The Kennedys solved that by arranging to have Gloucester mayor Benjamin A. Smith II appointed to the seat. A college pal of Jack's, Smith agreed to step down in 1962 when Teddy would be thirty, old enough to run for the Senate seat.

Joe then began to help his youngest son prepare for the campaign. Kennedy arranged trips overseas to help Ted understand foreign affairs, scheduled speaking engagements throughout Massachusetts so voters would meet his son, and introduced Ted to important political, business, and civic leaders. Ted also worked, for $1 a year, as an assistant district attorney in Suffolk County prosecuting criminal cases, which gave him experience at a real job.

Winning an Election

Kennedy announced his candidacy with much fanfare March 14, 1962, but just a few days later the *Boston Globe* reported his Harvard cheating incident. The revelation, however, did little damage to his campaign and he went into a vicious primary battle against

Edward McCormack gestures at Edward Kennedy during a debate in their U.S. Senate race. Kennedy won the election with the help of his family's wealth and influence.

Edward McCormack, who claimed, "If his name was Edward Moore, his candidacy would be a joke. Nobody's laughing when your name is Edward Moore *Kennedy*."[110]

The Kennedy name was his biggest asset, and even though McCormack had a solid record as Massachusetts attorney general and was the nephew of John McCormack, the powerful Democratic Speaker of the House, Kennedy crushed him in the September 19 primary by winning 69 percent of the vote. In the November 6 general election Kennedy beat George Cabot Lodge—a member of the same family Jack defeated to win his first Senate race—with 54 percent of the ballots cast.

His election meant the Kennedy family could now boast a president, attorney general, and U.S. senator. But the victory increased fears that this growing political dynasty was abusing the power it was accumulating, and an editorial in the *New York Times* claimed Ted's election was "demeaning to the dignity of the senate and the democratic process. . . . [The Kennedys] cannot see that, where the family was concerned, they applied the old nepotism."[111]

Because of such charges, the freshman senator kept a low profile and stayed away from Jack in public. However, Ted would often go to the White House when his Senate day was done to swim and relax with Jack. Those visits, however, would not last long.

Another Assassination

The day his brother was killed Ted was presiding over a session of the Senate, a typical duty for a freshman legislator. When Jack's

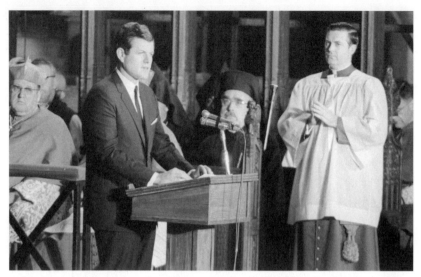

Edward Kennedy delivers the eulogy at the funeral mass for his brother, Robert. Kennedy was devastated by the loss of a second brother to an assassin's bullets.

assassination was reported, the shocked younger brother flew to Hyannis Port to be with his parents the next day. With his sister Eunice, he told their father that his son was dead.

Like the rest of the Kennedys, Ted was in a daze during the next few days of his brother's funeral and national mourning. But another death five years later was even harder on him. In *The Last Brother*, Joe McGinniss writes that Bobby's death devastated Ted more because, "All his life, at the bad times, it had been Bobby to whom he'd reached out. And almost always, Bobby had been there for him. Bobby was his greatest source of strength, of solace."[112] Ted pulled himself together for the funeral, however, and delivered Bobby's eulogy in New York City's St. Patrick's Cathedral: "My brother need not be idealized, or enlarged in death beyond what he was in life. He should be remembered simply as a good and decent man, who saw wrong and tried to right it, saw suffering and tried to heal it, saw war and tried to stop it."[113]

Ted was credited with giving a magnificent speech under difficult circumstances, but afterward his grief overwhelmed him. He withdrew from public life for several weeks, going on long sails and drinking heavily as he mourned his brother's death. He ignored pleas from Democrats to take over his brother's antiwar campaign and run for president, saying he simply could not do it. "I have never seen any human being so devastated," said Richard Drayne, his press secretary. "I thought to myself, 'How can that man ever be the same again?'"[114]

In late August, Kennedy finally came out of his self-imposed shell. He gave a speech at Holy Cross College in Worcester, Massachusetts, in which he criticized U.S. involvement in the Vietnam War and said he was returning to his Senate duties:

> Today, I assume my public responsibilities, like my brothers before me. I pick up a fallen standard. Sustained by the memory of our priceless years together, I shall try to carry forward that special commitment—to justice, excellence and to courage—that distinguished their lives.[115]

Although Kennedy had passed up an opportunity to run for president in 1968, his effort to carry that "fallen standard," which most people interpreted as the Kennedy family's virtual destiny to seek the presidency, got off to a good start in early 1969 when he was elected Senate assistant majority leader. Vigorously attacking the policies of Republican president Richard M. Nixon, who had defeated Humphrey, Kennedy grew in stature and came to be considered the Democratic Party's strongest 1972 presidential candidate. Despite this success, Kennedy biographer David E. Koskoff explains that Kennedy began to display personal weaknesses, which he attributes to an inability to cope with his brother's assassination: "Teddy started to come apart at the seams in 1969. His inclination towards wild driving became more pronounced. He began to drink seriously and heavily—the only one of the sons to show any weakness in that respect."[116]

On an airplane flight to Alaska in April 1969, for example, Ted drank heavily and expressed his own fear of being killed, muttering, "They're going to shoot [me] the way they shot Bobby."[117] His drinking, womanizing, and tendency to drive recklessly, which in college had earned him the nickname "Cadillac Eddie," would come together tragically to kill his presidential ambitions.

Chappaquiddick

In July 1969 Kennedy went to the island of Martha's Vineyard, Massachusetts, for a reunion of female staffers who had worked on Bobby's 1968 campaign. Shortly after 11 P.M. on July 18, Kennedy left a party on nearby Chappaquiddick Island with twenty-eight-year-old Mary Jo Kopechne. Kennedy's car accidentally ran off a small bridge and plunged into the water; Kennedy managed to escape from the vehicle but Kopechne did not, and drowned. In a police statement the next morning, Kennedy said:

> I was driving my car on my way to get the ferry back [from the island to Martha's Vineyard]. I was unfamiliar with the

road and turned onto Dyke Road instead of bearing left on Main Street. After proceeding for approximately a half mile on Dyke Road I descended a hill and came upon a narrow bridge. The car went off the side of the bridge.[118]

The situation, however, was not that simple. Unanswered questions lingered about why Kennedy and Kopechne had left the party together; whether Kennedy took Dyke Road so the couple could go to a secluded beach; his failed attempts (or lack of attempts) to rescue Kopechne; and his actions following the incident, including his failure to notify authorities until the next morning.

An investigation absolved Kennedy of any wrongdoing and he received tens of thousands of cards and letters supporting him despite the scandalous implications of the incident, but his reputation was tarnished forever, as were his presidential aspirations. In his 1999 biography of Kennedy, Adam Clymer states, "The accident at the bridge changed [his life], for the better and the worse, but forever. Chappaquiddick, as the voters understood it, excluded him from the Presidency he might have won."[119]

Troubled Personal Life

Chappaquiddick, however, was only one of a host of problems in Kennedy's private life. Ted and Joan had three children—Kara in 1960, Edward Jr. in 1961, and Patrick in 1967—but their marriage

Edward Kennedy is questioned by journalists during the inquest into the death of Mary Jo Kopechne. The incident destroyed Kennedy's chance to be elected president.

was rocky from the start because of his drinking and unfaithfulness. Kennedy biographer Lester David believes Joan, who herself battled alcoholism both before and after divorcing Ted in 1984, could not cope with the fact that her husband was seeing other women: "She was unlike Rose, who chose to ignore her husband's infidelities, and totally unlike Jackie, who was aware of Jack's escapades but never spoke about or confronted him about his affairs."[120]

The drinking and womanizing continued over the decades, and in early 1991 Kennedy was involved in another highly publicized and embarrassing incident. He spent that Easter at the Kennedy winter home in Palm Beach, with other family members including William Kennedy Smith, the son of his sister Jean. When Smith was charged with raping a woman he had met at a bar and brought back to the estate, Kennedy was caught up in the scandal; he had also been drinking at a bar with Smith that night and trying to pick up women himself.

Smith was eventually acquitted, but the incident again damaged Kennedy's reputation. By this time, he was physically bloated and grossly overweight, a caricature of the handsome young man he had once been. Realizing that he had to do something to save himself politically and personally, Kennedy in October apologized publicly for his tawdry lifestyle: "I recognize my own shortcomings, the faults in the conduct of my life. I realize that I alone am responsible for them and I am the one who must confront them."[121]

Kennedy had already begun to moderate his drinking and lead a healthier lifestyle, changes sparked by Victoria Reggie, whom he had begun dating in June. The thirty-eight-year-old Reggie was a lawyer and divorced mother of two teenage children—Curran and Caroline—whom Kennedy had known for years. Despite a twenty-one-year difference in their ages, they fell in love and were married July 3, 1992. The new relationship helped Kennedy lead a more stable life.

Kennedy's Legacy

As the twenty-first century began, Kennedy had been a senator for nearly four decades. And despite his personal problems, he was considered a fine lawmaker for his many legislative accomplishments and a prominent spokesman for the policies that had come to be associated with his family name, such as social welfare legislation and the need for America to play an active role in world affairs. He also became a leading and passionate advocate in the Senate for many liberal causes, including voting rights, fair housing, consumer protection, and a system of national health

*Edward Kennedy and his second wife, Victoria Reggie. The relationship
helped Kennedy lead a more stable life.*

insurance to make sure even the poorest Americans would receive
quality medical care.

Although Adam Clymer is critical of many aspects of his life, he
ends his biography of Kennedy with this assessment: "He deserves
recognition not just as the leading Senator of his time, but as one
of the greats in its history. . . . A son of privilege, he has always
identified with the poor and the oppressed."[122]

In his years as a legislator Ted, even more than Jack or Robert,
had won a reputation as someone who was willing to fight for the
disadvantaged. In a way, however, he was only following the
wishes of his father. In September 1940, Joe had written Ted from
London about the horror of the nightly bombing raids by German
planes. In the letter, Joe expressed the following wish for his
youngest child: "I hope when you grow up you will dedicate your
life to trying to work out plans to make people happy instead of
making them miserable, as war does today."[123]

Joe's wish came true; his words sum up Kennedy's career as well
as any ever written.

CHAPTER 5

Jacqueline Kennedy Onassis: Defender of the Kennedy Legacy

In the days and weeks following John F. Kennedy's assassination, the letters Jacqueline wrote to scores of friends ended with the appeal, "Please never forget him." It seemed an odd request to make about a political figure so unlikely to fade from the national memory, but Jackie was obsessed with how future generations would remember him. That was why, only a week after his tragic slaying, she invited Theodore H. White to Hyannis Port.

White, who met the Kennedys while writing *The Making of the President 1960*, arrived November 29 hoping to get enough information for a *Life* magazine article. Jackie stunned him with a soul-searing confession of her reaction to the assassination, facts and quotes he turned into one of journalism's most famous articles. It was during their long, emotional talk that Jackie compared her husband's presidency to King Arthur's reign in Camelot, a metaphor that the veteran journalist, at her passionate urging, only grudgingly accepted.

When White finished writing, Jackie demanded he make some changes in the story and suggested this new ending: "For one brief shining moment there was Camelot." When White dictated the article over the telephone, his editor wanted to cut that line. But Jackie refused, and it remained to help ignite the myth-making that would shroud her husband's presidency. Years later, White commented on how Jackie had manipulated him:

> It was no accident. She was a keenly intelligent woman who had obviously thought long and hard about how she wanted her handsome, heroic young husband remembered. She had always been described as a fairy-tale princess, and now she wanted Jack Kennedy to take his place in history as a modern King Arthur.[124]

By the time she died in 1994 at age sixty-four, Jacqueline Lee Bouvier Kennedy Onassis would be as well known worldwide as her husband. In his 1998 biography, Christopher Andersen writes:

> She held no high office, wrote no great books, created no masterpieces, performed no heroic feats. She invented nothing, discovered nothing. She had no interest in acting and could barely carry a tune. Yet she was the most celebrated American woman of the twentieth century.[125]

A Bouvier

She was born into a wealthy, Roman Catholic family on July 28, 1929, in Southampton, New York. Her parents were of French-American ancestry—John V. Bouvier III, who inherited money and was an investor, and Janet Lee. They divorced when Jackie was eleven for two reasons: Bouvier had lost most of his fortune in the 1929 stock market crash and Janet could no longer stand his drinking and infidelity. She then married wealthy investment banker Hugh Auchincloss.

Despite the unfaithfulness of her father, nicknamed "Black Jack" because of his dark good looks, Jackie loved him. "All my friends adored [her dad] and used to line up to be taken out to dinner when he came to see me,"[126] she once bragged of his visits to Miss Porter's School in Farmington, Connecticut, the exclusive school she began attending at age fifteen. She and her sister, Caroline Lee, who was three years younger, were brought up in wealth and luxury in New York, and at Miss Porter's, Jacqueline—a name she pronounced in the French fashion, Zhock-LEEN—had her own horse. When the slim, dark-haired beauty was eighteen, she was presented as a debutante to Newport, Rhode Island, society, and crowned Deb Queen of the Year.

Her mother's decision to divorce her father wounded the young girl but taught her two bitter lessons that would influence her life. The first was about how husbands behave. "I don't think," Jackie would later say, "there are any men who are faithful to their wives."[127] Author Gore Vidal, a friend and relative by marriage, claims the other lesson was the need to have a rich husband:

> Nothing, and I mean *nothing*, mattered more to Jackie than money. You must realize that this was the one thing Janet Auchincloss pounded into the heads of her daughters. She married Jack for money and she married Ari [Aristotle Onassis] for money.[128]

The Camera Girl

Jackie went to Vassar for two years, studied in Paris at the Sorbonne, and finished her schooling at George Washington University in the nation's capital. To the surprise of family and friends, she then began working as the Washington *Times-Herald*'s "Inquiring Camera Girl" for $42.50 a week, asking questions and taking pictures of celebrities. Retired *Times-Herald* photographer Joe Helberger, who taught her how to operate a Speed Graphic camera, said coworkers joked with her: "We'd say, 'Jackie, find yourself a rich one while you're out there.' She'd just smile."[129]

Five-year-old Jacqueline Bouvier in 1934 with her parents, John V. Bouvier III and Janet Lee.

Her April 21, 1953, column included a picture of John Kennedy and his whimsical observation that "I've often thought that the country might be better off if we Senators and Pages traded jobs."[130] But she had already met Kennedy in 1952 at a dinner party given by Charles Bartlett, a socialite and journalist. The Kennedys have always liked to embellish their personal history, and Jack would later tell biographers how he leaned over a dish of asparagus to ask her for a date. Years later, Jackie admitted, "There was no asparagus."[131]

But there was an attraction and Kennedy, a dozen years older, began dating the twenty-two-year-old beauty. Their early relationship was often conducted long distance because he traveled so much; Jack even proposed to her in a telegram. Jackie once said:

> It was a very spasmodic courtship. We didn't see each other for six months. . . . Jack began his summer and fall campaigning in Massachusetts. He'd call me from some oyster bar up there, with a great clinking of coins, to ask me out to the movies the following Wednesday in Washington. He wasn't the candy-and-flowers type, so every now and then he'd give me a book.[132]

They were married September 12, 1953, in St. Mary's Roman Catholic Church in Newport.

A Kennedy Wife

Jackie discovered it was not easy being a Kennedy. The family had always relegated its wives and daughters to secondary, supporting roles and she did not like being stuck at home while Jack campaigned or was busy with other duties. "I was alone almost every weekend," she said of their early years. "It was all wrong. Politics was sort of my enemy and we had no home life whatsoever."[133]

The new bride also struggled to establish a place in her husband's large, competitive family. Jackie and Rose barely tolerated each other and she hated the games the Kennedys constantly played, especially touch football, which she gave up in 1955 after Ted fell on her ankle, breaking it. This elegant young woman also was at odds with Jack's sisters, calling them the "rah-rah girls" and once claiming, "When they have nothing else to do, they run in place. Other times, they fall over each other like a pack of gorillas."[134] The Kennedy sisters, who blocked and tackled Jackie so hard in her first football game that she was black and blue, ridiculed the way she pronounced her name, her large feet (her shoe size was ten and a half), and her lack of athletic ability.

This portrait of John and Jackie Kennedy and his parents, Joseph and Rose, was taken in 1960, the year John was elected president.

One Kennedy she liked was Joe. They both loved classical music and would sit together for hours listening to records, and she could also make him smile. Once after she arrived late for lunch, a grievous sin for a Kennedy, Joe began to lecture her. She then startled family members by kidding him about his old-fashioned language: "You ought to write a series of grandfather stories for children, like 'The Duck with Moxie' and 'The Donkey Who Couldn't Fight His Way out of a Telephone Booth.'"[135] There was a hushed silence as the Kennedys braced for a burst of anger from the family patriarch. Instead, Joe began laughing.

The 1960 Campaign

Jackie eventually realized she was going to have to become involved in Jack's political life, and it was in his 1960 presidential campaign that Mrs. Kennedy became known in her own right. The media praised her beauty and poise, and Kennedy biographer William Manchester explains how she wooed voters during the Wisconsin primary:

John and Jackie Kennedy wave to the crowd during a campaign motorcade in New York City in 1960. The public loved seeing both Kennedys.

In Kenosha she entered a supermarket, listened to the manager announcing bargains over his public-address system, gave him a warm smile, and asked would he mind if she said a few words. The next voice the incredulous shoppers heard was Jacqueline Kennedy's: "Just keep on shopping while I tell you about my husband, John F. Kennedy." She talked, in her breathy but persuasive way, of his wartime service and his achievements [as a congressman]. She ended, "He cares deeply about the welfare of his country—please vote for him."[136]

Jackie's campaigning was limited, however, because she was pregnant with the couple's second child. Their first child, Caroline, had been born November 27, 1957, and John F. Kennedy Jr. arrived on November 25, 1960, a few weeks after his father was elected president. The expectant parents had watched election returns on television, and when it was apparent he would win, Jackie told him, "Oh, bunny, you're president now!"[137]

First Lady

At first, life in the White House was a shock to Jackie. "It was like a hotel," she complained. "Everywhere I looked there was somebody standing around or walking down a hall."[138] To escape the crush of people, she sometimes took her children to Glen Ora, the family home in secluded Middleburg, Virginia. But when she began to recognize the White House's historical and symbolic importance to the American people, Jackie worked hard to restore the Executive Mansion, redecorating and updating it while putting on display rare and beautiful antiques she found hidden away in storage. Her televised tour of the White House was broadcast live to an estimated 80 million people and earned her an Emmy Award.

Jackie brought a new aura of culture to the White House by hosting renowned artists such as poet Carl Sandburg and classical composer Igor Stravinsky. She reshaped women's fashion with her simple, elegant clothes, pillbox hat, and simple hairdo, all of which were copied by American women. But it was in her role as a mother that the public loved her the most, and magazines and newspapers were filled with pictures of her with John and Caroline.

Her campaigning success had made Jack realize his wife was a political asset, and he showcased her on foreign trips. The most memorable was their 1961 visit to Europe, where she thrilled both average people and world leaders. In Vienna, Austria, when photographers asked Soviet premier Nikita Khrushchev to shake hands with Jack, he pointed at Jackie and said playfully, "I'd rather shake hands with her."[139] At a luncheon in Paris, Jack noted his wife's new fame: "I do not think it altogether inappropriate to introduce myself to this audience. I am the man who accompanied Jacqueline Kennedy to Paris, and I have enjoyed it."[140]

Jackie Kennedy was a loving mother to her children, John Jr. and Caroline. This picture was taken in 1962.

Yet this storybook existence was underlined by sadness. Jackie's husband, like her father, was unfaithful.

A Troubled Marriage

Kennedy's infidelity was not revealed publicly until 1975 when Judith Exner Campbell, one of his mistresses, and others began disclosing his indiscretions. Asked once why he had continued such risky behavior while president, Kennedy answered truthfully, "Because I just can't help it."[141] Kirk LeMoyne Billings once noted,

"[Jack and Jackie] were both actors, and I think they appreciated each other's performances."[142]

Jackie was able to ignore Jack's liaisons with other women because she had learned as a child to disregard things that upset her, such as her parents' marital problems. "If something unpleasant happens to me," she once said, "I block it out. I have this mechanism."[143]

Perhaps Jack's most deplorable neglect occurred in 1956 after he lost his bid for the vice presidential nomination. Although Jackie was in the final months of pregnancy and there were concerns because she had suffered a miscarriage in their first year of marriage, Jack went on a cruise in the Mediterranean with Ted. While he was having fun, Jackie began to hemorrhage at their Hyannis Port home. She was taken to a hospital in nearby Newport, where doctors performed a cesarean operation August 12 and a baby girl was stillborn.

Jack could not be contacted for several days, an agonizingly long period for a woman to be alone after losing a baby. When Jack returned she was so angry that she threatened to leave him, remaining only after his father met with her and reportedly promised to give her $1 million. "Jack doesn't want to lose you," Joe told her. "I know your relationship hasn't been so hot, but you have to stick with Jack. He's going to be president."[144]

Yet it was the death of another infant, Patrick Bouvier Kennedy, which healed some of the bitterness between them. Weighing only five pounds and delivered six weeks prematurely on August 7, 1963, Patrick had severe respiratory problems and lived only thirty-nine hours. His parents grieved mightily over his death, and it was the first time Jackie saw her husband cry. Journalist Ben Bradlee is one of many people who believe that their shared grief over Patrick's death brought them closer together. Bradlee said the new relationship was evident at a party that September to celebrate their tenth wedding anniversary:

> This was the first time we had seen Jackie since the death of little Patrick, and she greeted [her husband] with by far the most affectionate embrace we had ever seen them give each other. They are not normally demonstrative people, period.[145]

The Kennedys, however, did not have much time left together. Two months later, he was assassinated.

Grace in Tragedy

It was in the days after her husband was killed in Dallas on November 22, 1963, that Jacqueline became a national icon, the

Just hours after her husband was killed, a grim-faced Jackie Kennedy watches Lyndon B. Johnson take the oath of office for president aboard Air Force One.

beautiful, tragic, yet composed widow of America's slain president. Seated next to her husband when he was shot, Jackie cradled him in her arms as the limousine rushed to the hospital and stood by his side while medical personnel tried to save his life. When doctors asked her to leave, fearing she might be upset by what they were doing, she refused: "His blood is all over me. How can I see anything worse than I've seen."[146]

When her husband was declared dead and she was left alone with his body, Jackie kissed him good-bye, took off her wedding ring, and tenderly placed it in his coffin. On the way to the airport for the flight back to Washington, Jackie was asked if she wanted to change out of her pink suit, which was stained red and bore bits of brain matter. "It's his blood," she said. "I do not want to remove this. I want them to see what they've done to him."[147]

Back home, Jackie began planning her husband's funeral, which she had decided should be like that of Abraham Lincoln, assassinated almost a century earlier. Jackie suggested the riderless horse that trailed his hearse to Arlington National Cemetery, the eternal flame that would forever light his grave, and the bagpipers Jack loved who played at his funeral. She also ordered the remains of their stillborn, unnamed baby girl and son Patrick to be buried next to their father.

While a nation and a world watched in awe, Jackie moved calmly and regally through the torturous weekend. Tens of millions of television viewers were amazed by the president's widow, who never faltered in the superhuman dignity she maintained. On the day of the funeral, a British journalist wrote the ultimate compliment to her stunning grace under pressure: "Jacqueline Kennedy has today given her country the one thing it has always lacked, and that is majesty."[148]

Two days after the funeral, she went to Hyannis Port to talk with Joe, who could not attend the funeral because of the stroke he had suffered two years earlier. Handing him the flag that had draped his son's coffin, she said, "Grandpa, Jack is gone, and nothing will ever be the same again for us. He's gone, and I want to tell you about it."[149]

The Widow

Before long Jackie realized how different her life would be now that her husband was dead. When she left the White House for a home in Georgetown, an exclusive residential area in the nation's capital, well-wishers and the morbidly curious gathered by the hundreds in front of the house, taking away her privacy. "I'm a freak now. I'll always be a freak," she told a friend. "I can't take it any more. They're like locusts, they're everywhere."[150]

Celebrity would stalk her the rest of her life, but Jackie found some relief from curiosity seekers by moving in 1964 to New York City, where she bought a five-room, fifteenth-floor apartment she kept for the next three decades. New York is a large city, one in which famous people can more easily lead a private life. The large dark glasses she now wore in public became a personal trademark, but they also helped her hide from prying eyes. "It may be that they're looking at me, but none of them can ever tell which ones I'm looking back at. That way I can have fun with it," she said.[151]

The one person Jackie could count on was the person she called "Saint Bobby," Robert F. Kennedy. "He's the one I'd put my hand in the fire for,"[152] she said of her brother-in-law, who had rushed to console her in 1956 after her stillbirth. A deep bond grew between them and they were together often, sometimes making private visits to Jack's grave late at night. They also worked together to preserve his memory.

The two were so close that speculation arose that they were lovers. But William Manchester, a family friend and biographer of John F. Kennedy, does not believe it: "An affair with Jackie would have been a violation of every moral fiber in Bobby's character. It would have been a desecration of his brother's memory."[153] Jackie was also dating other men after moving to New York, including actor Marlon Brando and cartoonist Charles Addams.

A chain-smoker until she finally quit in 1987, Jackie also drank heavily for several years following the assassination. She was able to control this problem in later life, but one skill Jackie never acquired was how to manage money. She had quarreled with Jack about how much she spent on clothes, as much as $20,000 a year, but as his widow she no longer had that much money. Although Jack's estate was worth more than $10 million, most of it was in trust funds for their children and her annual income was only $200,000; a lot of money for most people, but not someone with Jackie's expensive tastes.

Jackie "O"

She first met Aristotle Onassis in 1955 when the Greek tycoon hosted the Kennedys on his fabulous yacht, the *Christina*. In 1963 Onassis invited Jackie and her sister, now Princess Lee Radziwill after marrying European royalty, on an Aegean cruise to help her recover from Patrick's death. Onassis was squat, unattractive, and almost three decades older, but he had great personal magnetism and a fortune of over $500 million.

When Onassis began courting her she could not resist, and they married on October 20, 1968. In Onassis, who was so wealthy

Jackie Kennedy, with her children and brother-in-law Robert F. Kennedy at her side, greets England's Queen Elizabeth at a ceremony on May 14, 1965, to unveil a memorial to John F. Kennedy.

that he owned his own island, Jackie saw the security that her mother had taught her she needed for herself, as well as for her children. The Greek tycoon employed a large staff of security people, and many people believe that part of Jackie's motivation in marrying him was to provide more protection for her children. "If they're killing Kennedys, then my children are number-one targets,"[154] Jackie said after Robert Kennedy was assassinated. Four months later she married Onassis.

Newspapers around the world expressed shock at what they believed was her greedy betrayal of her dead husband. Soon known as "Jackie O," she fell out of U.S. public opinion polls listing the most revered women and she was harshly criticized by many people.

The marriage, in any case, was unhappy from the start. Jackie was in New York most of the time raising John and Caroline and she exceeded the $30,000 allowance Onassis gave her each month. Onassis had wed her to increase his social stature, but soon became upset by the huge sums of money she spent. "I thought I was buying a prize cow when I married Jackie," he once cruelly said. "How could I know the cow would cost me $50 million."[155]

Onassis became so bitter that he decided to divorce Jackie, but before he could go through with his plan he died in March 1975 of pneumonia and complications following an operation to re-

Jackie Kennedy and Greek multimillionaire Aristotle Onassis were married on October 28, 1968. Newspapers began referring to her as "Jackie O."

move his gall bladder. When Jackie flew to Europe for his funeral, she held a news conference in which she tried to put their relationship in a favorable light:

> Aristotle Onassis rescued me at a moment when my life was engulfed with shadows. He meant a lot to me. He brought me into a world where one could find both happiness and love. We lived through many beautiful experiences together which cannot be forgotten, and for which I will be eternally grateful.[156]

Onassis's death made her rich because she received $26 million from his estate. Widowed twice, it was time for Jackie to write the final chapter in her life.

Happiness at Last

Now in her midforties, her children teenagers, Jackie began to live a quieter existence out of the spotlight of the media, which had hounded her relentlessly during her volatile years with Onassis. Although Jackie now had money of her own, she became bored and decided to get a job. She worked part-time as a book editor, first for Viking Press and then for Doubleday, and her own celebrity helped her persuade stars like Michael Jackson to write their memoirs. Stephen Rubins, her Doubleday boss, said she was a hard worker:

> She was directly involved in everything—line editing, trim size, jacket designs, sales and marketing. She would call up a big book chain to push her books. And she was never grand [to people she worked with]. She would wait outside your office if you were on the phone.[157]

Jackie had always been close to her children, but the bonds deepened as she spent more time with them. When Caroline married and had children, Jackie reveled in her new role as grandmother to Rose, Tatiana, and John. Magazines and newspapers that formerly had pictures of Jackie cavorting on a yacht now ran photos that showed her at Caroline's wedding, with John at a Kennedy family gathering, or attending a charity event. There were men in her life, but the romances were low key and her main companion was Maurice Tempelsman, a wealthy diamond merchant. They were a couple for more than a decade even though he was married; his wife refused to divorce him. In her last twenty years, Jackie once again became one of the world's most admired women, which is why there was such a tremendous outpouring of

Arm in arm with good friend Maurice Tempelsman, Jackie Onassis walks in New York's Central Park with her daughter, Caroline, and Caroline's young son.

grief when she died May 19, 1994, of non-Hodgkins lymphoma, a form of cancer.

Remembering Jackie

In death, the world remembered only the best parts of Jackie's life—her devotion to her children, the elegance and grace she brought to the White House, her bravery in the face of tragedy. When Ted delivered her eulogy at St. Ignatius Loyola Church in New York, he explained why Jackie will be remembered forever:

> During those four endless days in 1963, she held us together as a family and as a country. In large part because of her, we could survive and then go on. She lifted us up and, in the doubt and darkness, she gave her fellow citizens back their pride as Americans.[158]

CHAPTER 6

John F. Kennedy Jr.: Another Family Tragedy

John F. Kennedy Jr. must have found it strange to be remembered by tens of millions of people for a moment in his life for which he himself had no recollection. That moment was the touching salute the three-year-old gave his father's flag-draped coffin on November 25, 1963, following the slain president's funeral service in Washington, D.C. As the casket bearing John F. Kennedy's body was being pulled away from St. Matthew's Church on a horse-drawn caisson, an old-fashioned two-wheeled military vehicle, Jacqueline Kennedy knelt down and whispered, "John, you can salute Daddy now and say good-bye to him."[159]

Clad in a bright blue coat with two rows of buttons and short pants, John raised his right hand in a military salute to his father as the caisson slowly passed by. For people who were watching on television or saw photographs of him the next day in newspapers around the world, John's good-bye became one of the most indelible memories of the assassination. Richard Cardinal Cushing, who officiated at the funeral mass, was overcome by the moving farewell. "Oh, God," Cushing said, "I almost died."[160]

Yet John, who had turned three years old that day, retained no memory of his farewell salute. "I've seen that photograph so many times," he

John F. Kennedy Jr. salutes the casket bearing his slain father's body. This photo became one of the most indelible images linked to John F. Kennedy's assassination.

81

said wistfully in an interview three decades later, "and I'd like to say I remember that moment, but I don't."[161] But it was precisely because so many millions of people could not forget it that this small boy would always be remembered himself.

A Famous Baby

Fame was something he had from the day of his birth on November 25, 1960, Thanksgiving Day, a little more than two weeks after his father was elected president. A premature baby delivered seventeen days early by cesarean section, he weighed only six pounds, three ounces and spent his first six days in an incubator at Georgetown University Hospital in Washington, D.C. John was born with hyaline membrane disease, a milder case of the respiratory disease that would kill his newborn brother Patrick three years later, but the media was never told about the condition that threatened his life those first few days.

His father was away when John became the first child born to a president-elect; he had flown to Palm Beach, Florida, to consult with his own father on cabinet appointments. Remembering his absence in 1956 when Jackie gave birth to a stillborn girl, Kennedy was hard on himself for being gone again. "I'm never there when she needs me,"[162] he told friends. Since the birth of Caroline three years earlier, Kennedy had become a loving father, and he was disappointed he had missed his son's birth.

John F. Kennedy Jr. peeks out from beneath his father's desk in the White House Oval Office. John often played in his father's office.

John was only a few months old when he became the first infant in the White House since President Grover Cleveland's daughter Esther was born in 1893. Within a year he was roaming the Executive Mansion with his dad, endearing himself to journalists who loved taking his picture and writing stories about his antics. Jack realized that articles about John and Caroline could boost his popularity, but Jackie tried to shield them from too much attention. When a photographer wanted a picture of the children playing in John's bedroom for the White House *Guidebook*, she refused. "Gentlemen," Jackie said, "even at the age of two, one's bedroom should be private."[163]

But there were scores of other photo opportunities for John, who when he was older walked with his father each morning from the family residence portion of the White House to the Oval Office. There he would play beneath his dad's massive desk, which had been used by both Presidents Woodrow Wilson and Franklin D. Roosevelt. The desk had a sliding front panel from behind which John would peek at photographers, who eagerly took his picture, producing some of the most memorable, endearing shots of him as a toddler.

After a few minutes of play, Kennedy would tell John to leave. Once when his son refused, he decided to begin meeting with his staff anyway. When the president asked, "What have we got [to do] today?" the first answer came from beneath his desk, "I've got a glass of water."[164]

Father and Son

It was after one of their typical father-and-son encounters that a reporter incorrectly told the world that the president called his son "John-John," creating a nickname John would hate for the rest of his life. Historian William Manchester explains:

> One day the president left his Oval Office and called his son, who was playing nearby, "John." There was no response. Kennedy raised his voice, "John." This time the boy heard him, jumped up, and came on the run. A minor aide recounted the episode to a reporter who asked, "And what were the president's exact words?" The aide replied: "John! John!" By the time this reached print it had become "John-John." Reading it, Jack caustically remarked, "I suppose if I'd had to call him three times, he'd have become "John-John-John."[165]

Kennedy enjoyed teasing his children. During a Christmas break in 1962 in Palm Beach, Kennedy pulled his son's trunks down while John was getting out of a swimming pool and pushed him back in. "Naughty daddy," John said. When Kennedy did it again, the little boy shouted, "Daddy, you are a pooh-pooh head." Amused by his son, the elder Kennedy said, "John Kennedy, how dare you call the president of the United States pooh-pooh head. You rascal, wait until I get ahold of you."[166]

The president's son was fascinated by airplanes and helicopters. So Maud Shaw, the nanny who cared for John and Caroline, knew she could find him in the White House hangar once when he was late for lunch:

> Sure enough he was [there]. And so was the president. Both of them were sitting at the controls of the helicopter with flying helmets on. The president was playing the game seriously with his son, taking orders from Flight Captain John, thoroughly absorbed in the whole thing. I retreated quietly and left father and son very happy together.[167]

Because the president not only works but lives in the White House, Kennedy spent more time than ever with his family, and being around his children so much tempered his conduct as president. During the Cuban Missile Crisis, he told aide Dave Powers:

> If it weren't for the children, it would be easy to press the button [and fire missiles at Cuba]. Not just John and Caroline, and not just the children in America, but children all over the world who will suffer and die for the decision I have to make.[168]

Kennedy understood that if he miscalculated in responding to the dangerous situation, he could ignite a nuclear war with the Soviet Union. And just as his father had not wanted his sons to die in World War II, Kennedy did not want his children killed in a nu-

President John F. Kennedy applauds while John Jr. and Caroline dance with glee in the Oval Office. Kennedy loved playing with his children.

clear holocaust. His deft handling of the crisis prevented war, but he could not prevent another tragedy that would affect his son—his own assassination.

The Assassination

John was at the White House playing with a toy helicopter and Caroline was being driven to her first sleepover when news of their father's slaying reached Washington. When Jackie returned home, she could not bear to tell her children about their father. She and Jack had always come back from the airport by helicopter, however, and the two kept screaming excitedly, "Daddy is home!" whenever a helicopter landed to bring yet another official to the White House. When Jackie was asked who should tell them, she said, "I think Miss Shaw should do exactly what she feels she should do."[169]

Shaw gave the news to Caroline when she put her to bed that night. The next morning she told John, who was too young to understand. "Your father has gone to heaven to look after Patrick [who had died four months earlier]," Shaw said, to which John childishly responded, "Did daddy take the big plane [Air Force One] with him? I wonder when he's coming back."[170]

Hand-in-hand with their mother, John and Caroline attended many ceremonies in the two days before their father's funeral, which was on John's third birthday. Because Caroline's birthday was only a few days after his, Shaw gave them each a small gift the morning of the funeral and there was a party that night for both of them. Caroline's favorite present was a stuffed bear and John's a model of Air Force One.

On his birthday, John also gave his father one final gift. Before the funeral, John had seen some small flags representing various nations. "Please," he asked a security guard, "may I have one for daddy?"[171] John got several, one of which was placed in Kennedy's coffin.

Growing Up a Celebrity

John left the White House as the little boy millions of Americans had fallen in love with through pictures and stories that appeared during his father's presidency. For example, when photos showed that John's hair had grown almost as long as a little girl's, the public joined in the family debate over his hairstyle—his mother preferred it long, his father short—by sending cards and letters suggesting he get a haircut. Some people even sent money to the White House to help pay for a trim.

Life as a celebrity was not easy for the youngster even though the Secret Service, which had given him the code name Lark, helped protect him. Agents accompanied him everywhere, including trick-or-treating at Halloween and to his first rock concert when he was twelve, a performance by Bob Dylan and the Band at Madison Square Garden. The Secret Service tried to shield John from the media, but there was often nothing they could do. As a little boy he once glared at a group of photographers and cried out, "What are those silly people taking my picture for?"[172] Those "silly people" would trail John for his entire life, hoping to make money with the images of him they captured on film.

His Secret Service detail also went to school with John, following him on and off the bus he took when he was older. John began his education in 1965 at St. David's in Manhattan and later attended the Collegiate School for Boys in Manhattan and Phillips Academy in Andover, Massachusetts, a prep school from which he graduated in 1979.

His mother's marriage to Aristotle Onassis provided John with even more protection than the Secret Service could give him. John got along well with Onassis, who told him they were *filarcos*, Greek for "buddies," but the youth was never close to his stepfather. Although John had a close relationship with his uncle Edward, John never had a father figure in his life.

Remembering His Dad

On October 20, 1979, fifteen-year-old John accompanied Jackie and Caroline to Dorchester, Massachusetts, to dedicate the John F. Kennedy Library. Afterward John told his mother, "You know. I don't even remember him. Sometimes I think I might, but . . . I don't."[173] Jackie, however, did all she could to keep Jack's memory alive, including having friends like Pierre Salinger, her husband's press secretary, talk to her children. Salinger once explained his role:

> She wanted them to know he was a human being, not a myth. I thought it was important that they not be spoonfed all the Camelot stuff, that would just give them a warped, unrealistic view of President Kennedy. In the end, Caroline and John had a healthy perspective on their father. All the credit goes to Jackie.[174]

John also worked hard himself to keep his father's memory fresh. Family friend Charles Spalding remembers walking into a room while the teenager was playing a recording of a tribute his father had recorded to Eleanor Roosevelt, widow of President Franklin D. Roosevelt. John told him: "Listen, right in here is where I crawl under the desk and dad kicks me. It's coming up now. Here it is. He was talking on the radio and I crawled under the desk and grabbed him."[175]

Although John would always feel a deep sense of loss over his father's death, he was not a sad little boy or depressed young man. But occasionally there were bitter reminders of the past, such as in 1966 when Jackie picked him up at school on the anniversary of the slaying and heard another child yell at John that his father was dead. Jackie was shocked by the cruelty of the taunt but John took her hand and squeezed it, she said, "as if he were trying to reassure me that things were all right. And so we walked home together."[176]

Some Wild Times

The Secret Service tried to protect the youngster from such incidents and from the voracious appetite of the news media for pictures and stories of him. But as John grew older, his protectors began to seem to him more like guards. When he was thirteen, John slipped away from his Secret Service contingent so he could ride his bike alone in Central Park. But while John was pedaling his ten-speed, a man jumped out of some bushes and stole his bike. The mugger was caught, but Jackie did not press charges because the incident would have been so heavily publicized.

John was ecstatic in the fall of 1976 when he entered Phillips Academy because it meant he would have more freedom in his life. It was the first time he had left home to attend school and in

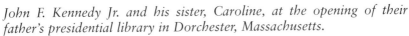

John F. Kennedy Jr. and his sister, Caroline, at the opening of their father's presidential library in Dorchester, Massachusetts.

John F. Kennedy Jr. and his sister, Caroline, chat during a ceremony to honor their father at Harvard University in 1978.

just a few weeks he would be sixteen, which meant the security detail mandated by federal law for all children of former president until that age would end. Like many teenagers, John had begun experimenting with alcohol and marijuana. When he was twelve he was caught drinking with some friends, and at Phillips he was punished several times for using drugs. But Holly Owen, his soccer coach and head of the school's drama department, claims he did not have a problem. "John smoked grass, but it didn't appear to affect him. I think his drug escapade was part of the rite of passage [of growing up]. When John experimented with drugs, it was only to be one of the boys, not because he was out of control."[177]

Seeking Adventure

Some Kennedy cousins, however, did have drug and alcohol problems. In 1984, David Kennedy, Robert's son, died of a drug overdose near the family estate in Palm Beach. Jackie tried to keep John and Caroline from spending too much time with their cousins, who she believed were spoiled. "She did not want her children caught up in the mystique of being a Kennedy,"[178] said Adrian Allen, a friend of Jackie's. Sensing her attitude, the younger Kennedys were often cruel to John, calling him a "mama's boy" and claiming he was not a "real Kennedy."

It was partly to keep John away from other Kennedys that Jackie began sending him on a series of summer adventures, which began in 1971 when he was ten. That first year he went to Wales to learn to sail, canoe, rock climb, and camp outdoors. In the next few years John would help earthquake victims in Guatemala, be taught to survive in the African jungle, and dive for sunken ships off Cape Cod. When he was a ranch hand in Montana in 1978, he was complimented by ranch owner John Perry Barlow: "I guess we expected another spoiled rich kid coming to spend a few weeks at the dude ranch. Instead, he was completely down to earth, a hard worker—just a real nice kid."[179] Barlow's perspective was shared by most people meeting John, who had impeccable manners and never flaunted his fame and wealth.

Like his father, John loved sports, particularly the more adventurous sort such as kayaking, skiing, and diving, and he was always testing his physical limits, which were superior. As an adult he was six feet one inch tall, weighed 175 pounds, and was a strong all-around athlete with great endurance and tremendous reserves of energy.

Breaking family tradition by attending Brown University instead of Harvard, Kennedy graduated in 1983 with a bachelor of arts degree in history and then spent nine months studying public health and education at the University of New Delhi in India. He returned home in June 1984 to work for the nonprofit 42nd Street Development Corporation, which his mother had founded, and nurse a dream of becoming an actor. To the dismay of his mother, he had performed in many school plays and in 1985 he tested himself professionally by accepting the male lead in *Winners*.

When Kennedy debuted on August 5, 1985, at Manhattan's tiny Irish Arts Theater, neither his mother nor sister would attend because they disapproved of his acting. After receiving some good reviews, Kennedy decided to attend Yale Drama School, but when he told his mother she was so angry that she gave him an ultimatum: "I'll disinherit you unless you go to law school."[180] He gave in, setting aside his dream of acting.

Prosecutor, Publisher

Kennedy attended New York University Law School in Manhattan from 1986 to 1989 but it took him three tries to pass the New York State bar exam. His failures earned him headlines like "The Hunk Flunks," a reference to his good looks, but he soon began working as a New York City assistant district attorney. Although Kennedy tried and won a handful of cases in four years, he did not enjoy being a prosecutor, claiming once that he would rather help criminals turn their lives around than put them in jail.

Kennedy also contributed his time to worthy causes, a lesson he had learned from his grandmother, Rose, before she died January 22, 1994, at the age of 104. Rose liked to quote this biblical passage from Luke: "For unto whomsoever much is given, of him shall be much required." Kennedy took the words to heart, volunteering in programs such as the Special Olympics for the physically and mentally disabled and Reaching Up, a foundation he started in 1987 to fund education for mental health–care workers. He was also involved in Kennedy family projects and in 1989 recorded an audiotape version of *Profiles in Courage* to benefit his father's memorial library.

Kennedy had trouble finding a job that interested him until he came up with an idea for a magazine that would focus on politics. At the news conference for *George*'s debut, he kidded reporters by saying, "I don't think I have seen as many of you in one place since they announced the results of my first bar exams."[181] In a letter from the editor in the first issue in October 1995, Kennedy explained that with *George* he wanted "to demystify the political process, to enable you to see politicians not just as ideological symbols but as lively and engaging men and women who shape public life."[182]

He did much more than lend his name to the magazine as its founder, writing articles and conducting interviews with controversial figures such as Cuban dictator Fidel Castro, his father's adversary in the missile crisis of 1962. He also worked hard to promote the magazine, including his comical appearance on the

His mother and sister accompany John F. Kennedy Jr. to his graduation from New York University Law School.

John F. Kennedy Jr. discusses George *magazine, which he founded, at a 1995 news conference to launch the publication.*

popular television show *Murphy Brown*, in which he gave the star a free subscription to *George*.

The cover of the first issue featured model Cindy Crawford dressed as George Washington, an irreverent shot that indicated the magazine would not be boring. A later cover was more controversial; actress Drew Barrymore dressed as Marilyn Monroe as she had looked when she sang a sexy version of "Happy Birthday" to Kennedy's father in 1962. The cover created a sensation because it reminded the world of his dad's affair with Monroe, and of his own highly publicized romantic life as well.

Marriage

Kennedy was so ruggedly handsome that *People* magazine in September 12, 1988, proclaimed him "The Sexiest Man Alive." The title brought him a lot of ribbing from friends, but as he once noted, "People can say a lot worse things about you than you are attractive and look good in a bathing suit."[183] And the public had seen lots of shots of Kennedy bare-chested, courtesy of the photographers who still pursued him so avidly. Only now these photographers were as interested in who Kennedy was with, because he was dating some of the world's most famous and beautiful women.

Magazines loved running lists of the celebrities Kennedy went out with including Crawford, actress Darryl Hannah, and rock star Madonna. Madonna early in her career had patterned herself after

Monroe, and it is believed she pursued Kennedy because she felt she was fated to have an affair with him because Monroe had one with his father. They dated briefly in 1985 and again in 1988 after she divorced actor Sean Penn, but the relationship was never serious.

Many biographers have noted that Kennedy, like his father and grandfather, loved being around sexy, beautiful women, especially famous actresses. The difference, however, was that Kennedy was single during his sexual escapades and, unlike them, he would take his marriage vows seriously when he did marry Carolyn Bessette. Bessette, a six-foot-tall, blue-eyed blond who graduated from Boston University in 1988 with a bachelor's degree in elementary education, had once posed for a "Girls of B.U." calendar. Instead of teaching, she modeled for a short time and then became a salesperson for Calvin Klein clothing in Boston and then New York.

Some biographers say the couple met in 1993 when Carolyn was assigned to help Kennedy shop at Klein's Manhattan store; others claim they first saw each other while jogging or in-line skating. Either way, they fell in love and were married September 21, 1996, in a small chapel on a remote island off the Georgia coast, far from the prying eyes—and cameras—of the media.

"I am the happiest man alive," Kennedy said the day he was married.[184] But the couple's happiness was short-lived.

Another Kennedy Tragedy

In 1998, Kennedy fulfilled his lifelong ambition to become a pilot. He had begun taking flying lessons a decade earlier, but quit after his mother begged him to stop because she was worried something would happen to him. The tragedy she had feared would occur on July 16, 1999.

On that night at 8:38 P.M., just after sunset, Kennedy took off from Essex County Airport in New Jersey in his Piper Saratoga. He and his wife and her sister, Lauren Bessette, were flying to Martha's Vineyard for the wedding of his cousin, Rory Kennedy. At 9:40 P.M. Kennedy's plane disappeared from radar screens tracking aircraft, and for the next few days, until the wreckage was finally found near Martha's Vineyard, the world waited in suspense to learn his fate.

His fame and family name made the personal tragedy a loss felt globally. As Ted admitted in the stirring eulogy for his nephew, "From the first day of his life, John seemed to belong not only to our family, but to the American family. The whole world knew his name before he did."[185] John's most dramatic claim to historical fame, the picture of him saluting his slain father, was reprinted in

John F. Kennedy Jr. and his wife, Carolyn Bessette. They were married only three years before their deaths in a plane crash.

newspapers and magazines in America and many other nations. The world's appetite for news of Kennedy was insatiable, and a *USA Today* editorial tried to explain this curious global fascination: "It's as if the family were our own. It is that intuitive personal connection, not the family's politics or its illusory fling at Camelot, that engages us. In the Kennedys we see ourselves."[186]

A Kennedy Curse?

Part of the world's fascination with the Kennedys has always centered on the many tragedies that have befallen them. Ted once raised the possibility that there was some "awful curse that hangs over all the Kennedys,"[187] and the media was all too happy to adopt his invention of a "Kennedy curse." John F. Kennedy Jr. once commented on the so-called curse, admitting, "It's sort of like walking around wondering if you are going to be struck by lightning."[188]

The lightning bolt finally struck. But the reality of life is that terrible things happen to every family; for all their talent, good looks, and wealth, the Kennedys are no more immune than any other clan to the human tragedy that is all too often a part of daily life.

NOTES

Introduction: The Kennedys: America's Political Royalty

1. Ronald Kessler, *The Sins of the Father*. New York: Warner Books, 1996, p. 3.
2. Quoted in Ralph G. Martin, *Seeds of Destruction: Joe Kennedy and His Sons*. New York: G. P. Putnam's Sons, 1995, p. xiii.
3. Quoted in Sidney C. Moody Jr., ed., *Triumph and Tragedy: The Story of the Kennedys*. New York: Associated Press, 1968, p. 30.
4. Quoted in Joe McGinniss, *The Last Brother*. New York: Simon and Schuster, 1993, p. 82.
5. Quoted in William Manchester, *Remembering Kennedy: One Brief Shining Moment*. Boston: Little, Brown, 1983, p. 273.

Chapter 1: Joseph Patrick Kennedy: Founder of a Political Dynasty

6. Quoted in James MacGregor Burns, *John Kennedy: A Political Profile*. New York: Harcourt, Brace & World, 1961, p. 6.
7. Quoted in Peter Collier and David Horowitz, *The Kennedys: An American Drama*. New York: Summit Books, 1984, p. 21.
8. Quoted in John H. Davis, *The Kennedys: Dynasty and Disaster*. New York: McGraw-Hill, 1984, p. 14.
9. Quoted in Richard J. Whalen, *The Founding Father: The Story of Joseph P. Kennedy*. New York: New American Library, 1964, p. 468.
10. Quoted in Davis, *The Kennedys*, p. 49.
11. Quoted in Whalen, *The Founding Father*, p. 43.
12. Quoted in Moody, *Triumph and Tragedy*, p. 7.
13. Quoted in Whalen, *The Founding Father*, p. 91.
14. Quoted in Arthur M. Schlesinger Jr., *A Thousand Days: John F. Kennedy in the White House*. Boston: Houghton Mifflin, 1965, p. 79.
15. Quoted in Doris Kearns Goodwin, *The Fitzgeralds and the Kennedys*. New York: Simon and Schuster, 1987, p. 351.
16. Quoted in Thomas C. Reeves, *A Question of Character: A Life of John F. Kennedy*. Rocklin, CA: Prima, 1992, p. 29.
17. Quoted in Martin S. Goldman, *John F. Kennedy: Portrait of a President*. New York: Facts On File, 1995, p. 4.
18. Quoted in Kessler, *The Sins of the Father*, p. 79.

19. Quoted in Collier and Horowitz, *The Kennedys*, p. 54.

20. Quoted in Reeves, *A Question of Character*, p. 44.

21. Quoted in Moody, *Triumph and Tragedy*, p. 46.

22. Davis, *The Kennedys*, p. 77.

23. Quoted in Whalen, *The Founding Father*, p. 285.

24. Quoted in Martin, *Seeds of Destruction*, p. 91.

25. Quoted in Goodwin, *The Fitzgeralds and the Kennedys*, p. 613.

26. Quoted in David Burner, *John F. Kennedy and a New Generation*. Boston: Little, Brown, 1988, p. 12.

27. Quoted in Moody, *Triumph and Tragedy*, p. 88.

28. Quoted in Whalen, *The Founding Father*, p. 465.

29. Goodwin, *The Fitzgeralds and the Kennedys*, p. 814.

30. Quoted in Moody, *Triumph and Tragedy*, p. 7

Chapter 2: John Fitzgerald Kennedy: The Son Who Became President

31. Quoted in Evan Thomas, *Robert Kennedy: His Life*. New York: Simon and Schuster, 2000, p. 39.

32. Moody, *Triumph and Tragedy*, p. 52.

33. Quoted in Kessler, *The Sins of the Father*, p. 287.

34. Quoted in Gail Cameron, *Rose: A Biography of Rose Fitzgerald Kennedy*. New York: G.P. Putnam's Sons, 1971, p. 119.

35. Quoted in Ralph G. Martin, *A Hero for Our Time: An Intimate Story of the Kennedy Years*. New York: Macmillan, 1983, p. 21.

36. Quoted in Goodwin, *The Fitzgeralds and the Kennedys*, p. 487.

37. Quoted in Martin, *A Hero for Our Time*, p. 36.

38. Quoted in Theodore Sorensen, *Kennedy*. New York: Harper & Row, 1965, p. 18.

39. Quoted in Robert J. Donovan, *PT 109: John F. Kennedy in World War II*. Greenwich, CT: Fawcett, 1961, p. 103.

40. Quoted in Donovan, *PT 109*, p. 127.

41. Quoted in Davis, *The Kennedys*, p. 125.

42. Quoted in Victor Lasky, *JFK: The Man and the Myth*. New York: Macmillan, 1963, p. 99.

43. Quoted in Manchester, *Remembering Kennedy*, p. 58.

44. Quoted in Moody, *Triumph and Tragedy*, p. 107.

45. Martin, *Seeds of Destruction*, p. 23.

46. Richard Reeves, *President Kennedy: Profile of Power*. New York: Simon and Schuster, 1993, p. 43.

47. Quoted in Collier and Horowitz, *The Kennedys*, p. 172.

48. Burns, *John Kennedy*, p. 113.

49. David E. Koskoff, *Joseph P. Kennedy: A Life and Times*. Englewood Cliffs, NJ: Prentice-Hall, 1974, p. vii.

50. Quoted in Sorensen, *Kennedy*, p. 135.

51. Theodore H. White, *The Making of the President 1960*. New York: Atheneum, 1961, p. 289.

52. Quoted in Goldman, *John F. Kennedy*, p. 85.

53. Quoted in Moody, *Triumph and Tragedy*, p. 178.

54. John Fitzgerald Kennedy Library and Museum, National Archives and Records Administration of the United States Government, University of Massachusetts, Boston, Mass., Text Archive. Available www.cs.umb.edu/jfklibrary.

55. Quoted in Sorensen, *Kennedy*, p. 495.

56. Quoted in Sorensen, *Kennedy*, p. 495.

57. John Fitzgerald Kennedy Library and Museum, National Archives and Records Administration of the United States Government, University of Massachusetts, Boston, Mass., Text Archive. Available www.cs.umb.edu/jfklibrary.

58. Quoted in Goldman, *John F. Kennedy*, p. 139.

59. Sorensen, *Kennedy*, p. 495.

60. Quoted in Martin, *A Hero for Our Time*, p. 568.

Chapter 3: Robert Francis Kennedy: The Third Son

61. Ralph de Toledano, *R.F.K.: The Man Who Would Be President*. New York: G. P. Putnam's Sons, 1967, p. 280.

62. Quoted in Moody, *Triumph and Tragedy*, p. 201.

63. Quoted in Goodwin, *The Fitzgeralds and the Kennedys*, p. 363.

64. Quoted in Richard D. Mahoney, *Sons & Brothers: The Days of Jack and Bobby Kennedy*. New York: Arcade, 1999, p. 10.

65. Quoted in Thomas, *Robert Kennedy*, p. 31.

66. Quoted in Martin, *Seeds of Destruction*, p. 102.

67. Quoted in Goodwin, *The Fitzgeralds and the Kennedys*, p. 364.

68. Quoted in Arthur M. Schlesinger Jr., *Robert Kennedy and His Times*, vol. 1. Boston: Houghon Mifflin, 1978, p. 63.

69. Quoted in Moody, *Triumph and Tragedy*, p. 61.

70. Quoted in Schlesinger, *Robert Kennedy and His Times*, p. 92.

71. Quoted in Thomas, *Robert Kennedy*, p. 61.

72. Quoted in Burns, *John Kennedy*, p. 114.

73. Quoted in Kessler, *The Sins of the Father*, p. 343.

74. Quoted in Mahoney, *Sons & Brothers*, p. 30.
75. Quoted in Moody, *Triumph and Tragedy*, p. 138.
76. Quoted in Schlesinger, *Robert Kennedy and His Times*, p. 96.
77. Thomas, *Robert Kennedy*, p. 191.
78. Lasky, *JFK*, p. 432.
79. Quoted in Schlesinger, *Robert Kennedy and His Times*, p. 242.
80. Quoted in Goldman, *John F. Kennedy*, p. 112.
81. Quoted in de Toledano, *R.F.K.*, p. 278.
82. Manchester, *Remembering Kennedy*, p. 233.
83. Martin, *A Hero for Our Time*, p. 419.
84. Toledano, *R.F.K.*, p. 16.
85. Quoted in Collier and Horowitz, *The Kennedys*, p. 312.
86. Quoted in Collier and Horowitz, *The Kennedys*, p. 312.
87. Quoted in Moody, *Triumph and Tragedy*, p. 204.
88. Mahoney, *Sons & Brothers*, p. 306.
89. Lester David, *Good Ted, Bad Ted: The Two Faces of Edward M. Kennedy*. New York: Carol, 1993, p. xii.
90. Quoted in Mahoney, *Sons & Brothers*, p. 317.
91. Quoted in Thomas, *Robert Kennedy*, p. 389.
92. Quoted in Moody, *Triumph and Tragedy*, p. 242.
93. Quoted in Thomas, *Robert Kennedy*, p. 303.
94. Quoted in Thomas, *Robert Kennedy*, p. 303.

Chapter 4: Edward Moore "Ted" Kennedy: The Last Son

95. Quoted in Lester David, *Good Ted, Bad Ted*, p. 26.
96. Quoted in James MacGregor Burns, *Edward Kennedy and the Camelot Legacy*. New York: W. W. Norton, 1976, p. 33.
97. Quoted in Martin, *Seeds of Destruction*, p. 25.
98. Quoted in Burns, *Edward Kennedy and the Camelot Legacy*, p. 35.
99. Quoted in Martin, *Seeds of Destruction*, p. 26.
100. Quoted in Goodwin, *The Fitzgeralds and the Kennedys*, p. 638.
101. Quoted in McGinniss, *The Last Brother*, p. 155.
102. Quoted in Martin, *Seeds of Destruction*, p. 104.
103. Quoted in David, *Good Ted, Bad Ted*, p. 40.
104. McGinniss, *The Last Brother*, p. 204.
105. Quoted in David, *Good Ted, Bad Ted*, p. 42.
106. Quoted in McGinniss, *The Last Brother*, p. 235.
107. Quoted in Koskoff, *Joseph P. Kennedy*, p. 467.

108. Quoted in Martin, *A Hero for Our Time*, p. 439.

109. Quoted in Goodwin, *The Fitzgeralds and the Kennedys*, p. 807.

110. Quoted in Burns, *Edward Kennedy and the Camelot Legacy*, p. 90.

111. Quoted in Whalen, *The Founding Father*, p. 478.

112. Quoted in McGinniss, *The Last Brother*, p. 38.

113. Quoted in Adam Clymer, *Edward M. Kennedy: A Biography*. New York: William Morrow, 1999, p. 118.

114. Quoted in David, *Good Ted, Bad Ted*, p. 10.

115. Quoted in David, *Good Ted, Bad Ted*, p. 12.

116. Quoted in Koskoff, *Joseph P. Kennedy*, p. 474.

117. Quoted in Martin, *A Hero for Our Time*, p. 572.

118. Quoted in Burns, *Edward Kennedy and the Camelot Legacy*, p. 165.

119. Clymer, *Edward M. Kennedy*, p. 605.

120. David, *Good Ted, Bad Ted*, p. 98.

121. Quoted in Clymer, *Edward M. Kennedy*, p. 502.

122. Clymer, *Edward M. Kennedy*, p. 609.

123. Quoted in Goodwin, *The Fitzgeralds and the Kennedys*, p. 609.

Chapter 5: Jacqueline Kennedy Onassis: Defender of the Kennedy Legacy

124. Quoted in Christopher Andersen, *Jackie After Jack*. New York: William Morrow, 1998, p. 75.

125. Andersen, *Jackie After Jack*, p. 434.

126. Quoted in "Daddy's Girl," *People Commemorative Issue*, Summer 1994, p. 21.

127. Quoted in Kessler, *The Sins of the Father*, p. 382.

128. Quoted in Andersen, *Jackie After Jack*, p. 176.

129. Quoted in "Daddy's Girl," p. 21.

130. Quoted in Herbert S. Parmet, *Jack: The Struggles of John F. Kennedy*. New York: Dial Press, 1980, p. 260.

131. Quoted in Kessler, *The Sins of the Father*, p. 344.

132. Quoted in Moody, *Triumph and Tragedy*, p. 118.

133. Quoted in Goodwin, *The Fitzgeralds and the Kennedys*, p. 772.

134. Quoted in Edward Klein, *All Too Human: The Love Story of Jack and Jackie Kennedy*. New York: Pocket Books, 1996, p. 121.

135. Quoted in "Into the Clan," *People Commemorative Issue*, Summer 1994, p. 35.

136. Quoted in Manchester, *Remembering Kennedy*, p. 93.
137. Quoted in White, *The Making of the President 1960*, p. 18.
138. Quoted in Martha Duffy, "A Profile in Courage," *Time*, May 30, 1994, p. 33.
139. Quoted in Martin, *A Hero for Our Time*, p. 353.
140. Quoted in Manchester, *Remembering Kennedy*, p. 186.
141. Quoted in Martin, *Seeds of Destruction*, p. 240.
142. Quoted in Goodwin, *The Fitzgeralds and the Kennedys*, p. 770.
143. Quoted in Klein, *All Too Human*, p. 34.
144. Quoted in Klein, *All Too Human*, p. 220.
145. Quoted in Parmet, *Jack*, p. 337.
146. Quoted in Duffy, "A Profile in Courage," p. 29.
147. Quoted in Martin, *A Hero for Our Time*, p. 558.
148. Quoted in Peggy Noonan, "America's First Lady," *Time*, May 30, 1994, p. 26.
149. Quoted in Kessler, *The Sins of the Father*, p. 413.
150. Quoted in Edward Klein, *Just Jackie: Her Private Years*. New York: Ballantine, 1998, p. 65.
151. Quoted in Andersen, *Jackie After Jack*, p. 434.
152. Quoted in de Toledano, *R.F.K.*, p. 13.
153. Quoted in Klein, *Just Jackie*, p. 88.
154. Quoted in Evan Thomas, Dorinda Elliott, and Richard Turner, "Living with the Myth," *Newsweek*, July 26, 1999, p. 38.
155. Quoted in Andersen, *Jackie After Jack*, p. 277.
156. Quoted in Klein, *Just Jackie*, p. 283.
157. Quoted in Duffy, "A Profile in Courage," p. 37.
158. Quoted in Clymer, *Edward M. Kennedy*, p. 542.

Chapter 6: John F. Kennedy Jr.: Another Family Tragedy
159. Quoted in Christopher Andersen, *The Day John Died*. New York: William Morrow, 2000, p. 78.
160. Quoted in David, *Good Ted, Bad Ted*, p. 86.
161. Quoted in Andersen, *The Day John Died*, p. 78.
162. Quoted in Goodwin, *The Fitzgeralds and the Kennedys*, p. 806.
163. Quoted in Michael Druitt, *John F. Kennedy Jr.: A Life in the Spotlight*. Kansas City, MO: Andrews McMeel, 1999, p. 70.
164. Quoted in Andersen, *The Day John Died*, p. 53.
165. Quoted in Manchester, *Remembering Kennedy*, p. 252.

166. Quoted in Reeves, *President Kennedy*, p. 441.

167. Quoted in Druitt, *John F. Kennedy Jr.*, p. 67.

168. Quoted in Martin, *A Hero for Our Time*, p. 462.

169. Quoted in Andersen, *Jackie After Jack*, p. 28.

170. Quoted in "The White House Years," *People Weekly Tribute: Commemorative Issue*, Summer 1999, p. 5.

171. Quoted in Stephen Spignesi, *J.F.K. Jr.* Secaucus, NJ: Carol, 1999, p. 6.

172. Quoted in Druitt, *John F. Kennedy Jr.*, p. 89.

173. Quoted in Andersen, *The Day John Died*, p. 163.

174. Quoted in Andersen, *Jackie After Jack*, p. 267.

175. Quoted in Martin, *A Hero for Our Time*, p. 573.

176. Quoted in Andersen, *Jackie After Jack*, p. 147.

177. Quoted in Andersen, *The Day John Died*, p. 154.

178. Quoted in "Fiercely Protected," *People Weekly Tribute: Commemorative Issue*, Summer 1999, p. 20.

179. Quoted in Andersen, *The Day John Died*, p. 159.

180. Quoted in Spignesi, *J.F.K. Jr.*, p. 23.

181. Quoted in Spignesi, *J.F.K. Jr.*, p. 11.

182. John F. Kennedy Jr., "Editor's Letter," *George*, October/November 1995, p. 10.

183. Quoted in "Boy to Man," *People Weekly Tribute: Commemorative Issue*, Summer 1999, p. 34.

184. Quoted in "The Most Eligible Bachelor and His Bride," *Time*, July 26, 1999, p. 41.

185. Edward M. Kennedy, "He Had Amazing Grace," *Newsweek*, August 2, 1999, p. 20+.

186. "Once Again, Tragedy Links Nation to the Kennedys," *USA Today*, July 19, 1999, p. 16A.

187. Quoted in Rick Hampton, "A Life, and a Family, Framed by Tragedy," *USA Today*, July 19, 1999, p. 5A.

188. Quoted in "John on John," *People Weekly Tribute: Commemorative Issue*, Summer 1999, p. 83.

CHRONOLOGY

April 21, 1849
Patrick Kennedy arrives in Boston, Massachusetts, from Ireland.

September 6, 1888
Joseph P. Kennedy is born.

October 7, 1914
Joseph P. Kennedy and Rose Fitzgerald are married by William Cardinal O'Connell.

July 28, 1915
Joseph P. Kennedy Jr., the couple's first child, is born.

May 29, 1917
John F. Kennedy is born.

November 20, 1925
Robert F. Kennedy is born.

July 28, 1929
Jacqueline Lee Bouvier is born.

February 22, 1932
Edward M. "Ted" Kennedy is born.

July 2, 1934
Joseph P. Kennedy becomes the first chairman of the Securities and Exchange Commission.

January 5, 1938
Joseph P. Kennedy is appointed ambassador to Great Britain.

August 1, 1940
John F. Kennedy's *Why England Slept* is published.

December 2, 1940
Joseph P. Kennedy resigns as ambassador to England.

August 2, 1943
PT 109, commanded by John F. Kennedy, is sunk by a Japanese destroyer; eight days later he and his crew are rescued.

November 5, 1946
John F. Kennedy wins his first election, for a seat in Congress to represent part of Boston, Massachusetts.

November 4, 1952
John F. Kennedy defeats incumbent Henry Cabot Lodge Jr. for a U.S. Senate seat.

September 12, 1953
John F. Kennedy marries Jacqueline Lee Bouvier.

May 6, 1957
John F. Kennedy wins the Pulitzer Prize for biography for *Profiles in Courage*.

November 8, 1960
John F. Kennedy is elected president of the United States; in his inaugural speech January 20, 1961, he inspires Americans by telling them to "ask not what your country can do for you; ask what you can do for your country."

November 25, 1960
John F. Kennedy Jr. is the first child born to a president-elect; he becomes the first infant to live in the White House since President Grover Cleveland's daughter Esther in 1893.

October 22, 1962
John F. Kennedy announces a naval quarantine to halt the Soviet Union's missile buildup in Cuba; Soviet leader Nikita Khrushchev subsequently withdraws the missiles after a showdown with the United States.

June 22, 1963
John F. Kennedy proposes the Civil Rights Act, the most sweeping civil rights legislation in U.S. history.

November 22, 1963
John F. Kennedy is assassinated in Dallas, Texas.

November 29, 1963
Journalist Theodore H. White interviews Jacqueline Kennedy, and his famous magazine article touches off the "Camelot" myth-making of the slain president's life.

November 3, 1964
Robert F. Kennedy is elected U.S. senator representing New York.

June 5, 1968
Only hours after winning the California primary to strengthen his bid for the Democratic Party's presidential nomination, Robert F. Kennedy is assassinated in Los Angeles.

October 20, 1968
Jacqueline Kennedy shocks the world when she marries Greek tycoon Aristotle Onassis on the island of Skorpios.

July 18, 1969
Edward M. Kennedy drives a car off a bridge on Chappaquiddick Island; a passenger, Mary Jo Kopechne, is killed in an incident that destroys his presidential ambitions.

May 19, 1994
Jacqueline Lee Bouvier Kennedy Onassis dies.

July 16, 1999
John F. Kennedy Jr., his wife, Carolyn, and sister-in-law are killed when the plane he is flying to Martha's Vineyard, Massachusetts, crashes into the Atlantic Ocean.

FOR FURTHER READING

James MacGregor Burns, *John Kennedy: A Political Profile*. New York: Harcourt, Brace & World, 1961. Written in cooperation with Kennedy before the 1960 presidential election, it is one of the seminal works on his early life.

Adam Clymer, *Edward M. Kennedy: A Biography*. New York: William Morrow, 1999. A solid look at Kennedy's life by a reporter who has written about him extensively over the years for the *New York Times*.

Robert J. Donovan, *PT 109: John F. Kennedy in World War II*. Greenwich, CT: Fawcett, 1961. The best book written on the World War II experiences of Kennedy.

Doris Kearns Goodwin, *The Fitzgeralds and the Kennedys*. New York: Simon and Schuster, 1987. A very detailed look at how these two Irish immigrant families prospered in America and eventually succeeded in having one of their own elected president.

Sidney C. Moody Jr., ed., *Triumph and Tragedy: The Story of the Kennedys*. New York: Associated Press, 1968. Written by reporters and editors of the Associated Press wire service, this book is a readable account of John F. Kennedy's life and death, but fails to offer penetrating insights into Kennedy, either as a man or a political figure.

Stephen Spignesi, *J.F.K. Jr.* Secaucus, NJ: Carol, 1999. A scrapbook format with interesting information and pictures, but no continuous story line.

Evan Thomas, *Robert Kennedy: His Life*. New York: Simon and Schuster, 2000. A well-written and -researched biography that objectively tries to assess Kennedy's life.

Michael V. Uschan. *The Importance of John F. Kennedy*. San Diego: Lucent Books, 1999. This biography explains why Kennedy was a significant figure in U.S. history, revealing both the good and bad parts of his complex personality.

WORKS CONSULTED

Books

Christopher Andersen, *The Day John Died*. New York: William Morrow, 2000. The author's third book on the Kennedy family is authoritative and packed with solid details about John F. Kennedy Jr.'s life.

———, *Jackie After Jack*. New York: William Morrow, 1998. A readable account of Jackie's later life by an author who has written several books on the Kennedys.

David Burner, *John F. Kennedy and a New Generation*. Boston: Little, Brown, 1988. A balanced look at Kennedy that does not ignore his flaws. It gives the reader a thorough understanding of his personality and his effect on the events of his time.

James MacGregor Burns, *Edward Kennedy and the Camelot Legacy*. New York: W. W. Norton, 1976. The author had access to private papers and photographs in researching this biography.

Gail Cameron, *Rose: A Biography of Rose Fitzgerald Kennedy*. New York: G. P. Putnam's Sons, 1971. An adequate but uncritical look at the family matriarch.

Peter Collier and David Horowitz, *The Kennedys: An American Drama*. New York: Summit Books, 1984. An in-depth Kennedy family history from the time the president's ancestors immigrated to America.

Lester David, *Good Ted, Bad Ted: The Two Faces of Edward M. Kennedy*. New York: Carol, 1993. The author shows how the good and bad aspects of the personality of the youngest Kennedy have influenced his life.

John H. Davis, *The Kennedys: Dynasty and Disaster*. New York: McGraw-Hill, 1984. A look at the Kennedy family from founding father Joseph through the children of President Kennedy and his brothers and sisters.

Ralph de Toledano, *R.F.K.: The Man Who Would Be President*. New York: G. P. Putnam's Sons, 1967. A highly critical portrait of Kennedy written before the 1968 presidential campaign and the candidate's assassination.

Michael Druitt, *John F. Kennedy Jr.: A Life in the Spotlight*. Kansas City: Andrews McMeel, 1999. The basic facts of Kennedy's life accompanied by wonderful pictures of the subject throughout his lifetime.

Martin S. Goldman, *John F. Kennedy: Portrait of a President*. New York: Facts On File, 1995. A solid biography that relies on many sources to tell the story. Goldman is balanced in assessing the president's personality and his role in history.

Ronald Kessler, *The Sins of the Father*. New York: Warner Books, 1996. A detailed portrait of the Kennedy family patriarch. The author is critical of Kennedy's character flaws and explains how his behavior influenced the development of his children.

Edward Klein, *All Too Human: The Love Story of Jack and Jackie Kennedy*. New York: Pocket Books, 1996. The author, who knew Jackie Kennedy well, reports on their relationship, from the time Kennedy courted her through his death.

———, *Just Jackie: Her Private Years*. New York: Ballantine, 1998. A follow-up to his earlier book about the Kennedys, the author explores Jackie's life after her husband's death.

David E. Koskoff, *Joseph P. Kennedy: A Life and Times*. Englewood Cliffs, NJ: Prentice-Hall, 1974. An interesting, thoroughly documented biography of Kennedy that delves deeply into the darker side of his life and that of his children.

Victor Lasky, *JFK: The Man and the Myth*. New York: Macmillan, 1963. Written before the assassination, this is the first work highly critical of President Kennedy. The book describes in detail the political maneuvering of Kennedy and his father to get what they wanted—the presidency.

Richard D. Mahoney, *Sons & Brothers: The Days of Jack and Bobby Kennedy*. New York: Arcade, 1999. The author, who knew the Kennedy family, explores the relationship between the two brothers.

William Manchester, *Remembering Kennedy: One Brief Shining Moment*. Boston: Little, Brown, 1983. Manchester, a friend of John F. Kennedy's, provides a glowing tribute to Kennedy's life. It glosses over his failings but is well-documented and captures Kennedy's personality.

Ralph G. Martin, *A Hero for Our Time: An Intimate Story of the Kennedy Years*. New York: Macmillan, 1983. A readable biography that concentrates on John F. Kennedy's personal life, providing a sharp image of Kennedy the man.

———, *Seeds of Destruction: Joe Kennedy and His Sons*. New York: G. P. Putnam's Sons, 1995. The author explores the complex relationship between Kennedy and his sons and explains how he pushed them into realizing his dream of a Kennedy as president.

Joe McGinniss, *The Last Brother*. New York: Simon and Schuster, 1993. A critical look at Edward Kennedy, especially his troubled personal life.

Herbert S. Parmet, *Jack: The Struggles of John F. Kennedy.* New York: Dial Press, 1980. A well-documented biography that unmasks some of the myths surrounding Kennedy and treats him objectively.

Richard Reeves, *President Kennedy: Profile of Power.* New York: Simon and Schuster, 1993. An exhaustive, almost day-by-day account of Kennedy's presidency. Reeves had access to documents released long after Kennedy's death that shed new light on the decisions he made as president.

Thomas C. Reeves, *A Question of Character: A Life of John F. Kennedy.* Rocklin, CA: Prima, 1992. Just about every negative quote and story about Kennedy ever reported appears in this book. It destroys some of the myths surrounding Kennedy and provides valuable insights into his darker side, but is so unbalanced that at times the reader may question the author's credibility.

Arthur M. Schlesinger Jr., *Robert Kennedy and His Times,* Vol. 1. Boston: Houghton Mifflin, 1978. An exhaustive biography of Kennedy's early life.

——, *A Thousand Days: John F. Kennedy in the White House.* Boston: Houghton Mifflin, 1965. This memoir of Kennedy's presidency by one of his top aides won a Pulitzer Prize for biography. Despite providing fascinating details and insights into Kennedy's personality, it generally puts a positive spin on every event while ignoring Kennedy's flaws and mistakes.

Theodore Sorensen, *Kennedy.* New York: Harper & Row, 1965. This well-written biography by the man considered Kennedy's alter ego for many years articulates Kennedy's personality as few other books ever have. But Sorensen is too worshipful of his subject.

Richard J. Whalen, *The Founding Father: The Story of Joseph P. Kennedy.* New York: New American Library, 1964. One of the earliest biographies of the Kennedys, this book is exhaustively researched and presents a solid view of the senior Kennedy.

Theodore H. White, *The Making of the President 1960.* New York: Atheneum, 1961. The finest book on a presidential election ever written, it provides valuable detail and insight into how Kennedy became president.

Periodicals

"Boy to Man," *People Weekly Tribute: Commemorative Issue,* Summer 1999.

"Daddy's Girl," *People Commemorative Issue,* Summer 1994.

Martha Duffy, "A Profile in Courage," *Time,* May 30, 1994.

"Fiercely Protected," *People Weekly Tribute: Commemorative Issue*, Summer 1999.

Rick Hampton, "A Life, and a Family, Framed by Tragedy," *USA Today*, July 19, 1999

"Into the Clan," *People Commemorative Issue*, Summer 1994.

Edward M. Kennedy, "He Had Amazing Grace," *Newsweek*, August 2, 1999.

John F. Kennedy Jr., "Editor's Letter," *George*, October/November, 1995.

"John on John," *People Weekly Tribute: Commemorative Issue*, Summer 1999.

"The Most Eligible Bachelor and His Bride," *Time*, July 26, 1999.

Peggy Noonan, "America's First Lady," *Time*, May 30, 1994.

"Once Again, Tragedy Links Nation to the Kennedys," *USA Today*, July 19, 1999.

Evan Thomas, Dorinda Elliott, and Richard Turner, "Living with the Myth," *Newsweek*, July 26, 1999.

"The White House Years," *People Weekly Tribute: Commemorative Issue*, Summer 1999.

Internet

John Fitzgerald Kennedy Library and Museum, National Archives and Records Administration of the United States Government, University of Massachusetts, Boston, Mass., Text Archive. Available www.cs.umb.edu/jfklibrary.

INDEX

PICTURE CREDITS

ABOUT THE AUTHOR

Michael V. Uschan has written fifteen books including *America's Founders*, a multiple biography of George Washington, Thomas Jefferson, and other early American political leaders, and biographies of President John F. Kennedy and Minnesota governor Jesse Ventura. Mr. Uschan began his career as a writer and editor with the wire service United Press International. Journalism is sometimes called "history in a hurry." Mr. Uschan considers writing history books a natural extension of skills he developed in his many years as a working journalist. He and his wife, Barbara, reside in the Milwaukee suburb of Franklin, Wisconsin.